JENNINGS

THE MORAL CHILD

THE MORAL CHILD
—·—
Nurturing Children's
Natural Moral Growth

William Damon

THE FREE PRESS
A Division of Macmillan, Inc.
NEW YORK

Collier Macmillan Publishers
LONDON

The Free Press
A Division of Macmillan, Inc.
866 Third Avenue, New York, N. Y. 10022

Collier Macmillan Canada, Inc.

Printed in the United States of America

printing number

1 2 3 4 5 6 7 8 9 10

Library of Congress Cataloging-in-Publication Data

Damon, William
      The moral child : nurturing children's natural moral growth /
William Damon.
           p.   cm.
      Includes index.
      ISBN 0-02-906932-7
      1. Moral development.   2. Moral education.   3. Child rearing.
I. Title.
BF723.M54D36   1988
155.4′18—dc19   88-16543
                                                                              CIP

For Jesse, Maria and Caroline

Contents

Preface

———— • ————

Moral education has become a matter of widespread common concern. Parents worry that their children are growing up bereft of traditional values. Teachers complain that their students seem ethically shallow and worse. Responding to these worries, politicians have entered the act, demanding that schools devote more time and effort to moral instruction. Children's morality is no longer simply a question of conduct in the home and corner playground; nor is it reserved for the province of religious leaders and scholars. It is the focus of public scrutiny and debate, a recognized societal problem of the first magnitude.

The social conditions that have fostered this rising tide of concern about children's morality are plainly apparent to anyone exposed to the daily news. Scandals revealing the shoddy ethics of respected public figures are disclosed almost daily in the national media. Trusted government officials, esteemed political candidates, popular religious leaders, and admired financial tycoons have all fallen loudly from grace in full open view. Revelations have ranged from the mundane to the spectacular, covering a host of moral sins and indiscretions: theft and financial chicanery, adultery and sexual assault, dishonesty and hypocrisy of every sort. The ranks of the disgraced have included persons occupying the highest positions of responsibility in our society. It is little wonder that people are asking whether, in social life today, children are learning cherished moral values, and whether moral education in the schools is all that it should be.

Even more disturbing, the health and future prospects of our young are becoming endangered by the prevailing moral confusion. Older generations have always fretted about the sexual morality of younger generations, but today the stakes have grown more serious. I refer here to the increasing risks posed by the many sexually transmitted diseases now threatening youth; and I refer also to the less dramatic yet still astonishingly widespread epidemic of teenage pregnancy. These are consequences of sexual behavior that can quite literally rob young people of their futures. With such risks in the wings, the sexual morality of youth takes on an immediate air of urgency.

Another clear and present danger to the futures of our young is the impoverished educational atmosphere of today's schools. This condition, too, reflects a problem in moral education, because it is a condition brought about largely by the poor conduct of many young people themselves. Even the best of our schools have been tainted with violence, drug abuse, and other antisocial behaviors. Such problems make traditional misdemeanors like cheating (which still very much exists) seem mild indeed. Constant confrontations with students' disorderly conduct have forced many school districts on the defensive. Their agendas have been reduced from the pursuit of learning to the far less lofty goal of maintaining discipline and order. Again, one wonders about the state of children's values today and about whether it might be possible to instill a finer sense of morality in our youth.

It is not surprising, therefore, that children's morality has been thrown full force into the public arena: politicians of every stripe, cultural and religious leaders of all types, and editorialists from newspapers, television networks, and magazines have called for vigorous moral education in the home and in the schools. Here traditionalists have closed ranks with progressives in agreeing that conscience is as important a focus of education as cognition. In fact it seems that moral values have joined the "three r's" as something that unquestionably belongs to a proper schooling experience.

But if we follow this public discourse a bit further, past the question of "Is moral education important?" to "How should we do it?" and "Which values should we teach our children?" the consensus begins to break down. This is also not surprising. After all, as adults we often disagree profoundly with one another about matters of right and wrong. Naturally, this translates quickly into disagreements about moral messages for our youth. Some of us would emphasize the virtues of liberty and autonomy whereas others of us would emphasize the virtues of loyalty, obedience, and respect for authority; some would emphasize the values of equality and need whereas other would emphasize the values of merit and excellence;

some would emphasize self-assertion while others would emphasize self-denial; some justice, others mercy; and so on, across every moral polarity that one could imagine.

Sometimes lost in this moral discord, though, are the inevitable hopes and expectations that all civilized people hold for their young. No one wants to lose a child to drugs or to an incurable disease, nor to see that child's future prospects squandered by a poor education or a premature parenthood. All parents oppose their children's engagement in acts of violence and other forms of antisocial behavior, except in highly unusual circumstances such as a civil revolt. Most adults want to see a younger generation that is imbued with incontrovertible moral virtues like honesty, kindness, a sense of responsibility, and a sense of fairness. These are human basics that transcend everyday political debate.

The great irony of our contemporary fascination with moral education—and it is a tragic rather than amusing irony, since the stakes are so high—is that much of our energy is spent arguing about contentious issues of lesser importance rather than working with problems that we all should see as crucial and urgent. We have allowed moral education to become a politicized issue rather than treating it as the educational right and developmental need that it really represents for our children. So we argue about nuances of ethical choice rather than concentrating on how best to communicate the core, unquestioned values of our culture to the young.

Moreover, our recent spotlight on moral education has avoided the scientific study of children's morality. The prevailing assumption seems to be that moral education is best implemented simply by telling children what values are right for them, unaided by any systematic knowledge, strategy, or technique.

Scholarship often seems removed from the press of real events, sometimes because its message is obscure, sometimes because its conclusions are tentative or hypothetical, and sometimes because its focus is simply irrelevant to our everyday concerns. In fact, this is so often the case that many people reflexively relegate the fruits of scholarship to the ivory tower without much expectation that they can help us solve our common life problems. Nowhere does this happen as frequently as with scholarship in the social sciences. People rightly have a suspicion of experts in matters of human affairs, and they naturally wish to retain the ultimate powers of belief and choice for themselves. When it ventures beyond the "merely academic" into the realm of public debate and policy, scholarship in the social sciences takes on a presumptuous air.

But our legitimate caution in such cases can lead to a lamentable loss of opportunity. Scientific information can guide us both in defining and resolving our choices about moral education. It can do so by helping us understand the processes through which children acquire moral values in normal social life; by helping us recognize the origins of morality and the milestones of moral development; by helping us analyze problematic moral conduct when it occurs; and by suggesting to us strategies for effective moral instruction.

There is no question, therefore, that scientific research on children's morality has a great potential to aid us in our pressing desire to improve children's moral values. This is an untapped potential, however, because most of this research is either unknown to the public, ignored as irrelevant, or debunked as ivory-tower nonsense. To the extent that this research is reported in the popular press, it is often fatally misrepresented.

Popular debunkers come even from within the walls of academia. Harvard psychiatrist Robert Coles, for example, has recently written a book called *The Moral Life of Children*.[1] Coles's book consists mainly of his own impressions and experiences with some youngsters who face adversity with nobility and principle. Coles dismisses social-science theory as irrelevant to his observations since, he claims, social science has not recognized that children can have a strong moral sense of their own. Coles implies that current psychological work has drawn two mistaken conclusions concerning children's morality: (1) that morality arises only as a defense mechanism, derived from other personal needs and mental systems, and thus is forced on children after extended periods of conflict; and (2) that morality is an abstract, logical system that develops late in life, mostly among well-educated persons. After implying that these impoverished ideas capture the sum total of social-science knowledge today, Coles positions himself on the side of children and in opposition to this insensitive science that belittles their incipient moral awareness.

Science has an establishment air about it, and antiestablishment railings always have a certain popular appeal. But Coles is simply wrong in his portrayal of the present state of knowledge about children's morality. As a research psychologist, in reading Coles I have a reaction akin to that of an eighteenth-century astronomer being shown a stinging attack on the "prevailing" notion that the sun revolves around the earth. The polemic takes the right side, but its enemies have been dead for years. Further, the attack contributes little to the understanding of the day and does a disservice by misrepresenting a useful body of knowledge to many who are unfamiliar with it.

Coles is not alone in his skeptical attitude towards scientific studies of children's morality. As noted earlier, there are several legitimate reasons for this skepticism. But it is our society's loss if we refuse to inform ourselves of the best available knowledge on an issue that we all agree to be a present-day imperative. Coles to the contrary, there is wealth of recent scholarship showing full respect for young children's early moral capacities. Contemporary journals are chock-full of studies on children's sharing, kindness, honesty under stress, and every other imaginable moral virtue, concept, emotion, and sentiment of the young. This, in fact, has been one of developmental psychology's hottest topics over the past twenty years. Practically none of this recent work treats morality merely as a defense mechanism or as an abstract system beyond the grasp of children.

The airwaves today are full of worried debate about children's morality. Yet in all this debate there is practically no reference to the storehouse of knowledge that social science has gained on this subject over the past fifty years. In my own lifetime I have never witnessed a larger gap between public discussion and unutilized information. My assumption is that this gap reflects a general lack of awareness more than a conscious aversion to this storehouse of knowledge. I do not believe that, where our children's welfare is at stake, people wish to take a "know-nothing" orientation to a complex and critical matter like moral education.

Rather, I believe that the scholarly work on children's morality is obscure because it has remained embedded in academic journals and scattered throughout disparate professional writings. There is no single accessible source where one can discover what is known about children's morality and how this knowledge can be applied to moral education. This book's first purpose is to provide that information. Its second purpose is to present a new position on moral education. It is a position that is quite different than those that we usually hear in public forums; nevertheless it is one that derives directly from our best information about the processes that determine children's moral development.

In documenting the natural flourishing of morality during the childhood years, I will show how morality grows readily out of the child's early social experiences with parents and peers. It is through common activities like sharing and helping, as well as through universal emotional reactions like outrage, fear, and shame, that children acquire many of their deep-seated values and standards of behavior. Adult influence, too, plays a crucial role; but it is a role that is necessarily limited as well as mediated through the child's other life experiences.

In emphasizing the complex and intertwining processes of moral growth, I take an unusual position on the moral education concerns currently sweeping the nation. Advocates on one side of the public debate assume that children must be indoctrinated in moral values if they are to grow up as responsible citizens. Advocates on the other side would rather leave morality to the incipient goodness of the child's own nature. This book will take issue with both sides of such debates. It will do so by showing that indoctrination is ineffective and possibly counterproductive as a moral development tool, but that certain guided instructional experiences are important in enhancing children's moral awareness and strengthening their sense of moral responsibility.

Several people have helped me directly or indirectly with the preparation of this book. I am grateful to Jerome Kagan for making available to me early manuscript versions of chapters in an important book that he has recently edited (with S. Lamb) on the emergence of moral awareness.[2] I have profited from discussions with James Youniss, Diana Baumrind, Elliot Turiel, Carol Gilligan, and Richard Shweder, and I also have benefited from reading recent manuscripts that they have sent me. Ann Higgins helped me gather a wide assortment of instructional material from current moral education programs, all of which was useful for my own Chapter 8 review of "morality in the schools." I also enjoyed a discussion with Ed Wynne on this topic and was interested to learn more about his point of view. Laura Wolff has been a careful and insightful editor, and Nancy Eisenberg provided me with helpful comments on the manuscript. As always, Anne Colby has given me invaluable assistance, intellectual and otherwise, throughout this project.

THE MORAL CHILD

1

·

Moral Concerns from the Child's Perspective

From an early age, children are acutely aware of moral concerns. The sense of outrage that a four-year-old feels when pleading "That's not fair" to a sibling, parent, or friend can be every bit as intense as an adult's reaction to any violation of rights. The same child might also respond with deep concern and care to another's misery. Young children feel the sting of injustice and the pull of empathy. They also know about their responsibilities to be honest, fair, kind, respectful, and loyal to their families and friends.

This is not to say that young children are moral saints, born with an incipient purity of character. There is much more to children's social conduct than the drive to be good. Like their elders, children can be unfeeling, selfish, and even cruel. They are capable of intentionally harmful as well as helpful behavior. But—and this is the crux of the matter—morality is a fundamental, natural, and important part of children's lives from the time of their first relationships. It is not a foreign substance introduced to them by an outside world of people who know all the answers.

If this statement seems somehow surprising or unrealistic, it is because we inevitably see children's behavior from an adult perspective. We very often tend to attribute a child's conduct, whether good or bad, solely to the influence of the adults in the child's life. We look for the examples that adults have set for the child, lessons that may or may not have been provided, rules that may or may not have been enforced, punishments that may or may not have been administered, and so on. From such a perspective, morality originates outside of the child's experience and is transmitted to the child directly or indirectly through adult tutelage.

I do not wish to belittle the importance of adult influence in shaping childen's morality. This book, in fact, is largely about

1

ways in which adults can encourage finer forms of moral awareness in their children. But it is a mistake to think of morality as a set of external standards that adults somehow foist upon an unknowing or unwilling child. Such an assumption distorts our view of the very real and intense moral feelings that children experience on their own accord. It overlooks the spontaneous expressions of moral sentiment that children frequently display in both peer and family settings. As a consequence, it places a formidable barrier in the way of our attempts to communicate with children about moral values. In fact, I shall make the case in later chapters that most of our current moral education efforts fail precisely because of this mistaken yet pervasive assumption.

Morality arises naturally out of social relationships, and children's morality is no exception. Wherever there is human discourse and interpersonal exchange there will follow rules of conduct, feelings of care, and sense of obligation. Children participate in social relations very early, practically at birth.[1] Their moral thoughts and feelings are an inevitable consequence of these early relations and the others that will arise throughout life.

The particular quality of a child's moral reactions will be shaped by the nature of the child's relationships. All children's moral reactions are marked by the features of childhood as it is played out in the cultural settings where they live. In Western society, children's social lives differ in many important ways from adult social lives. For example, children in our culture do not work for a living, control only insignificant sums of money, have no say in the governance of society, and bear little responsibility for life-and-death necessities—shelter, food, health, and medical treatment. Children rarely find themselves engaged in the moral problems that accompany such concerns, other than through observations or second-hand sources like the media.

It is because our own adult moral reactions focus on issues remote to children that we often have trouble seeing children's morality on its own terms. Often this causes us to disregard the full depth of a child's moral sensibilities. Because children do not directly wrestle with the identical moral issues that consume our own energies, we may fail to recognize their special moral concerns and may even assume that morality does not occupy as important a part of their lives.

But, like adults, children have an elaborate social life from which troubling moral problems frequently arise. There are friends, family, and desired personal possessions to allocate. There are obligations in the home, like obeying and helping; and by mid-childhood there are work and conduct standards in the schools as well. There are also standards of society to which they must adhere, and there are authority figures that enforce these standards: even young children will be prevented from stealing, trespassing, vandalism, and so on.

As soon as children can communicate with others and can make inferences about their social communications, they have ready access to their culture's values and beliefs. This very likely happens quite early in life: psychologists are now locating communication abilities well back in the infant years.[2] Children's early access to cultural values enhances their firsthand sense of the moral problems that can arise in social relationships. Out of the rich mix of relationships, possessions, obligations, and communicated values in a child's early experience grows a living childhood morality with its own vital characteristics.

What kinds of particular moral problems do children face? Any person who remembers being a child probably will recognize the following puzzles: Must I tell my parents the truth about disobeying them when I know it will only get me into trouble? Should I invite over the kid next door just because she's lonely, when I would rather do something else with my time instead? Do I have to share all my things with my cousin just because he lent me his bike just once? My best friend copied my answers on the test: should I let her cheat, or should I tell on her? Why shouldn't I steal a copy of my favorite recording from this store, since the owners are so rich and I have so little money?

These typical childhood moral problems focus on honesty, fairness, and one's concern for others. If these general concerns seem like familiar moral issues to us, so they should. For although childhood morality is shaped and expressed through the particular features of the child's social world, it revolves around concerns that arise everywhere in human moral discourse. As children play out their relationships with friends and family, they experience many of the same moral sentiments that we recognize in ourselves.

Sometimes it takes dramatic circumstances to draw our attention to this deceptively simple fact. In his book *The Moral Life of Children*, Robert Coles offers a useful and informative account of his own enlightenment on the matter.[3] Coles recounts several occasions where he was taken aback by incidents of childhood nobility under trying conditions. He tells, for example, of a young black girl named Ruby who was continually taunted by crowds when she broke the color barrier in a southern school of the early 1960s. Out of her own deeply held convictions, Ruby chose to pray for her tormentors rather than to silently curse them in bitterness and hatred. Ruby believed that, rather than sink to the morally misguided levels of her oppressors, she should await a better future with patience and hope. "Ruby," Coles writes, "had a will and used it to make an ethical choice; she demonstrated moral stamina; she possessed honor, courage." Coles confesses that he was ill-prepared to take seriously the spiritual generosity of this young girl as she responded to animosity with understanding and forgiveness. Like many other adults (experts included, Coles writes), he had been blind to the full moral potential of the child.

In the present book we shall encounter many examples of early sharing, generosity, kindness, honesty under stress, loyalty, and other varieties of virtue in the young. We shall also encounter an astonishing range of moral thoughts and emotions in childhood, from simple shame at being caught red-handed in a forbidden act to complex weighings of abstract principles like justice and mercy. We will identify the conditions that foster moral belief and conduct, tackle the question of individual differences, and suggest ways to facilitate the child's moral growth.

But first we need to take up a more basic conceptual issue, namely the very meaning and domain of morality itself. This is one of those words that two people can use totally differently in the same conversation. I have heard, for example, three educators argue about whether morality should be taught in the classroom, only to watch the three later discover that the first party was referring to religious training, the second to sex education, and the third to civics lessons.

There is, of course, no single, universally accepted definition of morality. Philosophers have debated this for centuries, and will continue to do so for as long as there is intellectual discourse. This is more than a semantic issue: the way in which one defines morality will predetermine many of one's conclusions about ethical belief and conduct and about moral education as well. Socrates made this clear long ago. When Meno asked him whether virtue was gained through practice, learning, or nature, Socrates answered: "You must think I am blessed indeed to know how virtue is gained.

Far from knowing whether it is learned or inherited, I have no idea of what virtue is."

Neither this nor any other book could ever wholly resolve the philosophical debate about how morality is best defined. The functions and purposes that morality must serve around the world not only are infinitely varied but also, in many cases, are still being created. Ethical issues are arising in places where they have been least anticipated: the "basic science" lab that uses genetic engineering, to choose just one example. Morality is a living, evolving, multifaceted construct that will never be pinned down by any one set of rigid definitional criteria. Nevertheless, the lack of perfect consensus on the meaning of morality need not force us to use the term in unanalyzed blind confusion. The following statements accurately describe the manner in which morality has been conceptualized in studies of children's moral development:

1. Morality is an evaluative orientation towards actions and events that distinguishes the good from the bad and prescribes conduct consistent with the good.
2. Morality implies a sense of obligation toward standards shared by a social collective.
3. Morality includes a concern for the welfare of others. This means that moral obligations necessarily extend beyond the individual's unmitigated selfish desires. The moral concern for others has both cognitive and affective components and bears implications both for judgment and conduct.
4. Morality includes a sense of responsibility for acting on one's concern for others. Such responsibility may be expressed through acts of caring, benevolence, kindness, and mercy.
5. Morality includes a concern for the rights of others. This concern implies a sense of justice and a commitment to the fair resolution of conflicts.
6. Morality includes a commitment to honesty as a norm in interpersonal dealings.
7. Morality, in its breach, provokes perturbing judgmental and emotional responses. Examples of such responses include shame, guilt, outrage, fear, and contempt.

While neither exhaustive nor philosophically uncontroversial, this list covers most of the moral dimensions that social scientists have identified as critical in human development. These dimensions define the territory that this book will cover and each represent a wide range of moral behavioral, and emotional possibilities. Acts that seem right to one person may seem wrong to another, and acts that shame some individuals make others feel proud. Variability is such an intrinsic characteristic of human morality that many wonder if there is any regularity to it at all. The search for such regularity, of course, is what motivates those who would understand and foster moral growth.

In the study of children, there is one kind of variability that is of special interest: the changes in moral judgment and behavior that come about as the child grows older. These changes inform us about the normal course of moral development. They tell us what to expect and offer us guidelines for educational intervention. The study of moral development is very much the study of how aging alters children's ideas about right and wrong and, along with these ideas, their emotional and behavioral responses to moral concerns. It is here that social scientists have sought and found some basic regularity.

How do we go about charting regular developmental changes in children's morality? The task requires comparing the behavior of young and old. This is trickier than it may at first appear. The social life of the young is somewhat foreign to those who are doing the comparing (the relatively old). This leaves a great deal of room for misinterpretation and oversight. The child may express a moral belief in a way that escapes the view of the adult who is observing the child. Or the child may operate from such an unfamiliar framework that the adult fails to capture it in all of its integrity. Many times the discrepancy in frameworks does figurative violence to the child's perspective (and even real violence to the child), as when an adult mistakes a child's well-intentioned act for a punishable offense. These possibilities represent conceptual, methodological, and communicational problems that can pose serious obstacles to our understanding of children's morality. In fact, the history of child study is full of noteworthy explorations that ran aground on such obstacles.

In the late 1920s, a team of distinguished researchers led by Hugh Hartshorne and Mark May of Yale became puzzled by their failure to find consistent behavioral patterns in children's moral behavior.[4] They had tried to predict which children would act honestly and which children would cheat on a series of experimental tasks. The tasks were problems such as naming the capitals of all the states in the United States without looking them up or asking anyone; or placing marks accurately inside circles drawn on paper with one's eyes closed. For one index of cheating, the investigators surreptitiously looked to see which children disobeyed the adults' instructions and helped one other with the answers.

Hartshorne and May had begun their investigation with the reasonable hypothesis that moral character was already beginning to form during childhood. They expected to find that children who had learned to be honest would tend to act that way with some consistency. They also assumed that children who could recite moral standards like the Ten Commandments and the Boy Scout Code would tend to demonstrate such standards in their behavior more than children who could not recite such standards.

But despite dozens of studies and thousands of subjects in one of the largest-scale investigations of its time, the researchers found very little pattern in their results. Children who were honest in one situation would cheat in the next, and nothing in their conduct seemed to be very closely related to how much they knew about the Ten Commandments or the Boy Scout Code.

The investigators concluded that the low and null correlations in their studies meant that children's morality is contextually determined. Moral conduct, they came to believe, is brought about more by the demands of certain situations than by the child's training or character. If there were developmental or personality factors that led towards consistent moral behavior, these did not seem to be operative during the childhood years.

From the vantage point of our current knowledge we can dismiss these results as incompatible with a slew of findings about moral growth in the childhood years. As we shall see, there is by now ample evidence of consistency and regularity in children's moral behavior, and there are many indications that enduring aspects of character are indeed formed early. How, then, could Hartshorne and May's extensive investigation overlook such important patterns?

We would ask above all whether the children in this study saw the moral issues in the same way as did the experimenters. Did they understand that copying obscure answers to bizarre tests was to be considered cheating? Perhaps in the eyes of the children who copied (or who let others copy their answers) these acts were seen as helping friends and in turn being helped. In such a light, so-

called "cheating" could become an act of loyalty and cooperation!
In situations that pit children against unfamiliar adults, honesty
may not even be the salient moral issue for children, especially
when the experimenter's tasks have little to do with everyday
school problems and so may not be perceived as serious school
tests, with all the attendant issues of competition, grades, and
school authority. Is it possible, therefore, that the same acts that
represented dishonesty and cheating to adults might have represented honor and helping to children? That acts which adults assessed as immoral represented the conduct of conscious moral
choice to the children who performed them?[5] It may well be that
Hartshorne and May's experiment did tap a rich vein of childhood
morality, but that this vein was neglected in the search for the
type of "pay dirt"—compliance with adult standards—that adults
recognize more easily.

It is clear to us today that it is not easy for adults to penetrate
children's own ways of viewing moral issues. This is because acts
that have serious moral implications for adults may seem trivial in
the context of childhood social relations. We cannot simply assume that the moral meaning of actions stays the same throughout
the course of development.

It may seem odd to us today that anyone could take a child's
ability to recite by heart the Ten Commandments and the Boy
Scout Code as a good indicator of the child's moral knowledge;
yet in Hartshorne and May's time this seemed reasonable and appropriate. By now we have learned enough to doubt whether a
child's shaky memory of such rules bears any implications for the
child's tendency to be kind, honest, loyal, obedient, and fair. We
know that children do not need to accurately represent adult moral
codes in order to have a rich morality based on their own social
experience.

The lesson taught to us by Hartshorne and May's investigation
is that children's moral sensibilities are easy to overlook if we expect them to be expressed in behavior that conforms to our adult
standards. Children have their own social lives and may take seriously different interpersonal events than we do. They may, for
example, share our respect for the standard of trustworthiness, but
they also may consider it more important to be trustworthy with
a friend than with a strange adult making strange requests—particularly when these two events come in conflict, as in the Hartshorne and May experiments. The message is clear: Adults who

would understand children's morality must understand the significance of children's acts within the context of the child's world.
The reason this is so difficult is that developmental change has
long ago transformed the typical adult's interpretation of virtually
all moral issues.

This is a message that deserves special emphasis, because social
scientists are not the only ones who encounter the obstacles of
developmental change in understanding children's morality. Parents, teachers, ministers—in fact all adults who try to teach children moral lessons—run up against the same barriers. Often they
do so unaware that the collision has taken place. Such unawareness
can impair the adult's ability to communicate about moral issues
with the child even further. It even can lead to a lingering condition of mistrust in the adult's relationship with the child.

The following is a true story told to me by an elementary school
teacher after a talk that I had given on children's morality. The
background to this incident is the sometimes stormy national debate over religion in the classroom. The teacher's school was in a
local district composed of worshippers from many diverse reli-
gions. The local school board had decided that the best way to
ensure the protection of all beliefs was to prevent teachers from
offering religious opinions to their pupils. The board expressly is-
sued an edict to that effect. The young teacher in question, new
to the profession, had been advised of this rule in her preservice
training and had accepted it without question.

The incident began with a classroom science project in which
the teacher's first grade pupils were asked to raise some fish in a
controlled environment. Each child had a fish to care for. When
one girl's fish died prematurely, she wanted to know what would
happen to the fish now that it was dead. Would it come back to
life somewhere, would it still be happy, would it remember the
little girl who had cared for it? The teacher immediately recognized the religious implications of these questions. She simply reas-
sured the girl that the fish was in no pain and that they could bury
it outside in the school yard. She told the girl that they would
never see the fish alive again, and suggested that she raise a new
one.

The next day an irate principal called the teacher into his office.
How, he demanded, could the teacher tell her pupils that fish go
to heaven when they die? Apparently, the little girl had relayed to
her parents the story of her fish's death, but had embellished the

teacher's statements with some comments about heaven. The parents, who strongly believed in a spiritual discontinuity between persons and animals, objected to their daughter's learning in school that fish could have an afterlife.

The teacher told the principal that she had said nothing of the sort, and the incident soon passed without further consequence. But the teacher was left with lingering doubts about her pupil. She liked the girl, but could not help but wonder if the child had acted mischievously, in order to stir up some trouble. Was she perhaps dishonest by nature? Or did she hold some undisclosed grudge against the teacher? These uncomfortable questions mingled in the teacher's mind with her basic belief that the little girl was just a child, acting childishly. But why, then, the provocative miscommunication to her parents?

Developmental psychologists who have studied six-year-old moral reasoning have learned some reassuring answers to the teacher's questions. The girl's invention need not (and probably could not) have sprung from malicious mischief. Far more likely was its roots in the natural tendency of young children to embody abstract moral notions in concrete places or events. This tendency has been called "moral realism" by many who have studied children's morality.[6]

In attempting to understand the death of a valued loved one, the little girl turned to the helpful notion of an actual heaven where good creatures find their just reward. This, of course, is a concept widely available in our culture. It is also a concept easily understood by children accustomed to thinking of spiritual ideas in terms of material properties and physical places. In contrast, the young girl was less likely to be impressed by her teacher's cryptic answers about the fish's disappearance.

For the young girl, her parents' abstract distinction between the spirituality of humans and the nonspirituality of animals inevitably left something of a conceptual vacuum, no matter how well-grounded such distinctions may be in classic theology. The girl filled this vacuum in a creative manner characteristic of six-year-olds. This resulted in an embellished version of what the teacher had told her. Whether the girl realized that her version of the teacher's explanation did not match the teacher's is something we shall never know. But it is reasonable to conclude that the girl's story was more a function of a six-year-old's need to understand a confusing and disturbing event than of an inherent character flaw.

This conclusion is in line with the teacher's common-sense intuitions, but she had some nagging doubts nevertheless. The doubts arose from the unavoidable gap between the meaning systems of children and those of even the most sensitive adults. It is a gap that poses an obstacle to our understanding of children's behavior in general and children's morality in particular. But researchers have found some ways of bridging the gap, and as a result have come away with significant insights about the terrain on the other side. The following chapters chronicle these explorations and identify the lessons contained therein, which may guide us toward our common goal of an effective moral education for our young.

2

Empathy, Shame, and Guilt

The Early Moral Emotions

Positive feelings like empathy, sympathy, admiration, and self-esteem, and negative feelings like anger, outrage, shame, and guilt are all essential parts of our moral reactions to situations. When strongly experienced, they provide pressing incentives to act in accord with our standards. They affect our behavior in social situations as well as our interpretation of those situations. Often it is the perception of a uniquely moral sentiment like guilt or responsibility that makes us first aware of the moral demands of certain life situations.

Moral emotions also contribute to the long-term development of moral values. Children naturally experience many moral feelings in the course of their social engagements. As children reflect on these moral feelings, they question and redefine the values that gave rise to the feelings. Sooner or later the redefined values are tested through conduct, all of which gives rise to new feelings, new reflections, and further redefinitions of the child's moral code. This is the lifeblood of the moral development process.

Most scholars believe that moral emotions are a natural component of a child's social repertoire, and that the potential for moral-emotional reactions is present at birth. Some have gone even further in claiming that moral emotions constitute the one feature of morality that unites humans from all the world's diverse cultures. Jerome Kagan has written that ". . . beneath the extraordinary variety in surface behavior and consciously articulated ideals, there is a set of emotional states that form the basis for a limited number of universal moral categories that transcend time and locality."[1]

Kagan and other like-minded scientists look to emotions rather

13

than reasoning or logic for the elements of a universal morality. Kagan suggests five "candidates" for the core moral emotions: (1) fear of punishment, social disapproval, or failure; (2) empathy towards those in distress; (3) guilt over one's own callous or irresponsible behavior; (4) "ennui" from the *over*satiation of a desire; and (5) anxiety over the awareness of inconsistency between one's beliefs and one's actions.

These widely shared feeling states, Kagan believes, motivate the acquisition of virtues that resolve the tensions associated with such states. The particular virtues that arise must be adaptive to one's time and cultural setting. Thus in ancient Greece, the virtues of physical courage and wisdom were developed in response to the same emotional states that engendered prudence, charity, and self-restraint in Victorian-era New England.

How are such feeling states experienced by the child? Research on this question has entered the nursery itself in search of the earliest possible signs of a moral reaction. Indeed, precursory signs of empathy have been identified in infants as young as two days of age.

Babies often cry and emit other signs of distress at the sound of another baby's crying. We do not know, of course, whether these infants are simply mistaking the others' cries for their own discomfort. But even granting such an egocentric confusion, this initial distress is an important indicator of a spontaneous tendency to identify with another's discomfort. The baby hearing the crying feels no pain of its own, yet still shows displeasure. Here we see, in the primitive world of the crib, one human sharing another's burdens. This signals the advent of empathy, one of morality's primary emotional supports.

Empathy means reacting to another's feelings with an emotional response that is similar to the other's feelings. In an empathic response, one becomes pleased by another's joy and upset by another's pain. It is a natural response that can be found in very young children, yet it is by no means an automatic or universal one: if it were, we would not need to be admonished by prescriptive messages like the Golden Rule ("Do unto others as you would have them do unto you"). The key questions, then, are when can we expect empathy to arise spontaneously, and what can we do to further foster it?

Although empathy is experienced as a feeling state, it has a cognitive as well as affective component. In order to resonate to another's feelings, a child first must recognize accurately the other's feelings. The cognitive ability to discern another's inner psychological states is called *perspective taking*. Children at birth may attune themselves to another in a rudimentary way (as when infants cry at another's crying), but their skill in perspective taking initially is limited. It follows that the child's empathic responses, which rely on perspective taking for their cognitive base, increase in frequency and scope only as the child develops some cognitive sophistication.

The role of perspective taking in empathy can help us understand and predict the course of empathic responding throughout the child's development, because it is chiefly perspective taking, the cognitive component of empathy, that changes with age.[2] Newborns have the capacity for some purely affective empathic responses. These early feelings become the emotional cornerstone of prosocial behavior. But for effective moral action, the child must learn to identify a wide range of emotional states in others. Further, the child must acquire the ability to anticipate what kinds of action will improve the emotional state of the other.

Martin Hoffman calls the newborn empathic response "global empathy" because the infant cannot yet draw clear boundaries between the feelings and needs of the self versus the other.[3] Global empathy characterizes infants' reactions to others' distress through the first year or so of life. These reactions can be strong and heartfelt. Hoffman gives an example of an eleven-month-old who had to fight off her own tears, then sucked her thumb and buried her head in her mother's lap after she had seen another child fall and hurt himself. He quotes another psychologist's observation of this type:

> At nine months, Hope had already demonstrated strong
> reactions to other children's distress. Characteristically, she
> did not turn away from these distress scenes though they
> apparently touched off distress in herself. Hope would stare
> intently, her eyes welling up with tears if another child fell,
> hurt themselves, or cried. At that time, she was overwhelmed
> with her emotions. She would end up crying herself and
> crawling quickly to her mother for comfort.[4]

Not all infants, of course, cry every time someone else is hurt. In fact, many times an infant will stare at another's pain with simple curiosity, or even amusement. Global empathy, though commonly seen in young infants, is neither a consistent nor a universal phenomenon.

The first developmental milestone after the global empathy phase of early infancy occurs between the ages of one and two. At this time the infant's undifferentiated feelings of discomfort at another's distress grow into feelings of genuine concern. The infant now realizes that the others are independent beings in their own right, with their own unhappy feelings. Further, the infant may sense that these unhappy feelings in others may need attention and relief. The infant, however, cannot translate this realization into effective action.

We probably have all observed cases of well-meaning but clumsy attempts at comforting others on the part of infants who still have only a shaky awareness of others' own needs. For example, Hoffman observed a thirteen-month-old who was responding with empathic concern to a crying playmate. The empathic child brought his own mother to comfort the crying child instead of bringing in the child's mother, who was equally available. The intention was considerate and kind, but the solution missed the mark because of the empathic child's projection of his own needs onto the other infant, a reflection of the child's lingering cognitive egocentrism. In other similar cases, toddlers have been observed offering unhappy-looking adults their own beloved blankets or dolls for comfort.

By the end of the second year, children have a firmer grasp on others' needs and feelings as distinct from their own. Increasingly over the next few years they become aware that every person's perspective is unique and that someone else may have a different reaction to a situation than oneself. This awareness enables children to respond appropriately to another's distress. For example, a child by the age of six may realize that an unhappy person in some instances may rather be left alone than be helped. The child may then learn to wait for just the right moment to offer comfort and to make the offer in a manner that will not interfere with the person's sense of pride or privacy. In short, children now can make an objective assessment of the other's needs while putting themselves in the other's place in order to locate the true occasion for distress.

In late childhood (ages 10–12), there occurs one further development in the child's capacity for empathy. This is a newly emergent orientation of empathy for people who live in generally unfortunate circumstances. The child's concern now no longer remains limited to the feelings of particular persons in situations that the child directly observes. Rather, children expand the scope of their concerns to include the general conditions in which unfortunate people sometimes must live. The child begins to empathize with the general plight of life's chronic victims: the poor, the handicapped, the socially outcast. This new sensitivity may lead the child to engage in charitable and altruistic behavior. A few years later, it may impart a humanitarian flavor to the adolescent's emerging political and ideological views.

Norma and Seymour Feshbach, researchers from the University of California at Los Angeles, have devised techniques for measuring children's empathic responses.[5] The Feshbachs distinguish between the cognitive and affective components of empathy and have designed assessment procedures for each. The cognitive measures require children to match pictures of emotion-laden events with faces signaling appropriate affective responses. For example, a child will be shown a picture of people sitting at the bedside of a sick grandparent. The faces will be deleted from the picture. The child's task is to select a sad face from a display of choices.

There are also affective empathy measures that tap children's emotional responsiveness to videotaped vignettes. Children watch enactments of scenes in which a child actor displays basic emotions like pride, happiness, anger, fear, or sadness. The child observers are then asked to report their own responses while watching these episodes. The researchers make note of both the emotion that the children report (in particular how closely it matches that of the child actor) and the intensity with which the child experiences that emotion.

Such procedures, and other like them, have been used with children in the early to mid-childhood range. Generally researchers have found that children with strong empathic capacities tend to engage less in aggressive behavior than do children with lesser empathic capacities. There is also solid evidence that a child's ability to empathize is associated with children's tendencies to engage in prosocial acts such as helping and sharing.[6]

In older children and adolescents, empathic dysfunctions can create the conditions for serious antisocial behavior. Young people convicted of violent crimes often express their lack of feeling for their victim's distress. This can take several forms, all of which serve to promote or justify the violent act. For example, the young

criminal might focus on a real or imaginary offense that the victim
has committed. This "offense" provides a rationale for the violent
act because it enables the young criminal to "shut off" feelings for
the victim. One criminologist quotes a seventeen-year-old habitual
house robber as saying: "If I started feeling bad, I'd say to myself,
'Tough rocks for him. He should have had his house locked better
and his alarm turned on.'"[7]

Perhaps most chilling are statements of young criminals who
profess no feelings whatsoever for those whom they hurt. I recall
a *New York Times* interview with a thirteen-year-old convicted of
viciously mugging a series of older persons, one of whom was a
totally blind woman. The boy expressed only the regret that he
was caught, and went on to say that the blind woman was his victim of choice, since she at least could not provide a legal identification. When asked about the lasting pain that he had caused this
unfortunate woman, the boy was surprised at the question and responded, "What do I care? I'm not her."

Even in hardhearted delinquents may flicker a glimmer of empathy from time to time. The problem is that it is only occasionally
felt; and when felt, inappropriately expressed. One psychologist
who has studied this problem writes, "Empathy is available in most
offenders but is not readily elicited and tends to be either an isolated impulse or a mawkish sentiment. In either case, the empathy
is superficial and erratic; when it lingers it is readily suppressed by
self-centered motives or aggressive impulses."[8] Criminals who have
committed violent acts like murder and rape have been quoted as
saying that, while they felt nothing for their victims, they have at
times been moved by the plight of the needy in society. One violent criminal even said that at times he has felt bad about chopping
down living trees at Christmastime.[9] Such occasional empathic expressions are hardly enough to support a prosocial life; but they
may indicate a deeply buried capacity for empathy, however trun-
cated or underdeveloped.

We can conclude, therefore, that everyone may be capable of
responding empathically; but it is also clear that some persons do
so far more consistently than others. Like the capacity for empathy
itself, such individual differences in empathic responding show up
very early in life. Children as young as one and two respond differently to others' distress. Moreover, these differences between
individual children endure, at least through the early childhood
years.

In one study, some toddlers responded to distress in a classic empathic fashion, with an expression of feeling for the other and a direct (though sometimes ineffective) attempt to help.[10] Other toddlers, however, responded more with curiosity than with emotion. They looked and asked questions, expressing interest in the event rather than showing strong concern for the others' feelings. When these children chose to be helpful, however, they did so as effectively as their more emotive peers. Quite the opposite was true of the remaining children. Some showed a total lack of interest in the others' pain, withdrawing at any sign of discomfort or distress. Others actually became aggressive when another expressed suffering. They scolded or even hit the complaining victim.

Such very early differences in how, or even whether, children empathize with others certainly have implications for how easily particular children will adopt moral beliefs and conduct. They also raise the standard nature/nurture questions: Are some infants born more predisposed to empathy and moral behavior than others? Or do certain types of very early experience produce the diferences described above? Is it heredity or environment that causes some children to express a greater, a warmer, or a more consistent concern for other people's feelings?

Like all nature/nurture questions, the "either-or" format can never provide an adequate answer, and in fact misses the heart of the issue. Certainly there are both constitutional and experiential-factors that contribute to every individual child's empathic capacities. These are often inextricably joined in the child's personality development and cannot be isolated from one another, even for the sake of analysis.

The strongest claims about genetic bases of empathy have been made by researchers comparing identical with dyzygotic twins.[11] These researchers report that identical twins are more similar in their empathic qualities than are dyzygotic twins. They therefore conclude that genetic composition must play a role, since the parental environments of the two types of twins are generally the same. But these researchers' only means of assessing children's empathic capacities was through their *self-descriptions*, which of course are shaped by many types of social influence after birth. For identical twins, one source of marked social influence is the special manner in which they are looked at, attended to, dressed, communicated with, and talked about from the moment of birth on (not to mention the particular social dynamics of their own interactions with one another). Such social factors make a difference in how children view and describe themselves. Thus even in research findings intended to show a genetic base for empathy, we see the interplay of social forces. Needless to say, there is also a substantial body of research that more directly (and more intentionally) demonstrates the role of parental response and other social factors in shaping children's empathic natures.[12]

There are more productive questions than the standard "either/ or," heredity-versus-environment ones. For the purposes of understanding and improving children's morality, one far more productive question is: Given a child's current empathic capacities, what are the conditions that foster or retard further growth in these capacities?

The most direct way to approach this question is by trying to design means of encouraging children to be more empathic. Potentially such attempts also could lead to some practical solutions for social problems like moral apathy and delinquency on the part of the young. In one such attempt, the Feshbachs designed an empathy training program for elementary school children.[13] This program is a ten-week course during which the child performs role-taking and affect-identification exercises with an empathy "trainer" three times a week. In their first experiments with this program, the Feshbachs found that children who participate in this program show increased prosocial activity during the course of the training. It is not clear, however, how long such training effects last. The children also showed some decrease in their tendency to act aggressively, although no more markedly than did children who received nonempathic training in social problem solving.

Clearer and more powerful effects have been obtained by innovative methods using small group discussions to enhance delinquents' empathic motivation.[14] In this approach, the delinquent discusses his own antisocial reactions of anger and moral apathy in the context of peer and adult feedback. Actual problem incidents are recreated and analyzed by the group. These presentations themselves can be laden with emotion and are often experienced by the participants as genuine social conflicts. The therapist's goal is to create a setting in which the delinquent is unavoidably faced with the emotional results to others of his own behavior, thus learning to take moral responsibility for his actions. Gibbs quotes a description of one such program:

In Yochelson's program, the theme of the criminal's injury
to others always hangs heavily in the air. . . . Leroy
[a participant] experienced new waves of awareness and
then disgust as to the scope of the damage that he had
inflicted. . . . Beyond physical suffering and financial loss,
injury extends to the emotional damage, to the climate of fear
engendered in the aftermath of a crime, and to the disruption
of lives. A small violation has a far-reaching effect.[15]

Such methods are effective because they leave an emotional as well
as cognitive legacy for their participants. In the example above,
the therapist aimed to engender disgust for immoral acts in delinquents who had committed the acts.

The feeling of moral disgust engendered by the group encounter
is a moral component of guilt, which follows from an awareness
of why one's actions were indeed wrong in the first place. The
heart of this awareness is the recognition that injury has occurred
to others and, accompanying this recognition, an empathic response to the victim's distress. Group discussions between youth,
led by a supervisor trained in peer dialogue techniques, have
proven to be one of the few successful means now available for
helping troubled youth develop this kind of interpersonal awareness and empathy.

Morality, of course, is fueled by constraining forces external to
the individual, as well as by the positive, empathy-driven urge to
alleviate the distress of others. No doubt the earliest of these external forces is the parent-child relationship. But what is remarkable
about human morality is the tendency of humans to establish the
most effective constraints inside themselves. These internal forces
take the form of pressing and often overwhelming feelings of prohi-
bition. Such feelings act as effective sanctions against immoral behavior precisely because they require no direct external monitor-
ing. One does not need to be caught in the act in order to
experience intense shame or guilt.

Shame is a feeling of embarrassment that is experienced when
one fails to act in accord with perceived behavioral standards.
Some believe that the capacity for shame is generated in early confrontations with parents over affect-laden issues like toilet training.
Whether intentionally or not, parents often humiliate children in
the process of inducing them to use the potty. Children sense the

parent's disgust and disappointment at the child's defecatory "mistakes." The child reacts with embarrassment to such incidents. This provides the first occasion for the experience of shame.

Although the roots of shame lie in episodes where children feel humiliated in front of their parents, by middle childhood shame becomes less directly linked to such actual confrontations. No longer is observation or discovery by others an essential part of a shameful reaction. Rather, children can feel shame whenever they do not live up to their internalized ideals. An eight-year-old who wets his pants during a laughing fit will feel embarrassed and humiliated even if he manages to hide it from his parents and peers.

In general, however, shame always remains to some extent other-oriented. Even when it is removed from an immediate fear of discovery, it is still emotionally linked to the sense that, in the eyes of others, one's behavior is contemptible. In this regard it differs from guilt, which relies more exclusively on one's own evaluations rather than on the real or imagined evaluations of others.

Guilt begins later in childhood than does shame, and is considered the more autonomous and effective of the two morally constraining emotions. Freud and his followers were the first to speculate on the developmental origins of guilt. In psychoanalytic theory, guilt is the enduring outcome of the child's Oedipal situation. The psychoanalytic scenario has taken many forms, but the most general version goes like this: Children naturally experience both erotic and hostile feelings towards their parents. By early childhood they become aware that such feelings are antisocial and therefore forbidden. As a consequence, children become fearful that such feelings, if expressed, may result in the loss of parental love. Thus the child senses that such feelings must be repressed.

In order to accomplish the repression of these threatening feelings, the child must develop an inner means of controlling antisocial feelings. The natural solution is to identify with the parent, already an object of love for the child, and in the process to take on the parent's role as guardian of moral constraints. This means that the child will adopt both the standards of the parent (which, in turn, reflect those of society) and the parent's ability to punish violations of these standards. When the ability to punish violations is transferred from the parent to the self (and thus "internalized"), it takes the form of guilt. In this manner, the child has acquired the powerful inner enforcer of conscience.

Contemporary researchers have found several reasons to modify the psychoanalytic version of guilt development. For one thing, research has found little connection between children's fear of losing parental love and the acquisition of internal moral values. For another thing, guilt as an experienced feeling is not empirically correlated with the strength of the parent-child identification. Further, it is doubtful that children are capable of taking on the entire, complex system of parental values in one fell swoop by the age of five or six.[16] Moral development is more accurately characterized as a gradual process that entails continual additions, modifications, and revisions of the child's values and behavioral standards.

There is another, more basic question that has been raised about the psychoanalytic approach to both shame and guilt. In the way Freud characterized them, are these moral emotions a healthy addition to the child's internal life, or do they merely sow the seeds for future neuroticism? From Freud's own writings onwards, there is a surprising ambivalence about this issue within the psychoanalytic tradition. Both moral emotions are seen as serving the necessary social function of constraining individuals' destructive egoistic impulses, but they do so at a terrible price to personal happiness. Freud saw this as part of the bargain implicit in civilized life. We renounce our instinctual urges for the protections of collective living. As a result, we accept a lifelong burden of recurring conflict and discontentment. In a healthy adaptation to life, the conflict is minimized, and the benefits of socialization outweight the inevitable price of psychological discontent.

Because of this emphasis on the unpleasant inner consequences of shame and guilt, psychoanalysts generally have dedicated themselves to reducing the impact of these emotions on individuals' mental states. Erik Erikson's theory, for example, places shame in opposition to the development of autonomy, and guilt in opposition to the development of initiative.[17] Erikson argues that toddlers must acquire a sense of self-control in order to "stand on their feet" and energetically accept the next challenges of life. Shame and doubt, which first appear at the toddler stage, are the natural enemies of self-control, and threaten the young child's growing sense of free will. Similarly, guilt poses the greatest danger to the preschoolers' emerging sense of initiative a few years later. It can curb children's pride in their achievements and their exuberance in the face of their new-found physical and mental powers.

It is not necessary, however, to treat shame and guilt as neurotic anxieties that retard development and mitigate against personal happiness. In fact, many contemporary psychologists have argued that such a position places the discipline in curious opposition to the most effective human enforcers of morality, the powerful constraining emotions. A way out of this dilemma was found in the 1950s by Donald Miller and Guy Swanson.[18] Miller and Swanson studied school children's expressions of guilt in stories that they told and pictures that they interpreted. In contrast to the predictions of psychoanalytic theory, Miller and Swanson found not one form of guilt but three. Of the three, two had some Freudian overtones of conflictual and restricting anxiety; but the flagship form was an adaptive orientation towards self-criticism in service of the self's optimal relations with others. Miller and Swanson concluded that this *interpersonal* form of guilt was the version normally found in mature individuals.

If interpersonal guilt is indeed different from the neurotic variety that Freud and other psychoanalysts have observed in their clinical patients, we must look beyond the Oedipal conflict for its origin. It does not seem likely that a single tumultuous episode early in life, however dramatic, could give rise to both forms of guilt. An emotion with pathological overtones is not likely to share its source with a well-adapted social orientation. Further, the formation of interpersonal guilt in its most mature form requires psychological development extending well beyond the Oedipal years.[19]

Interpersonal guilt is closely linked with empathy throughout the course of development.[20] Like empathy, interpersonal guilt is a feeling of discomfort at another's distress. Empathic discomfort turns into guilt when one experiences the sense that one somehow caused the other's distress. In more indirect forms, guilt also can arise from the sense that one did not prevent the distress from happening, or from the sense that one did not do enough to relieve the distress once it occurred.

Empathy therefore is a prerequisite for interpersonal guilt, and the two share their origins in the child's initial awareness of another's pain. In the case of guilt, however, there also must be some intimation of personal responsibility. In childhood, this usually takes the form of a self-attribution of causality for the painful event. Because causality is a notion that presents some conceptual difficulty early in life, the development of guilt relies in part on the child's cognitive growth.

The infant's first guilt experience occurs around the end of the first year, when infants fully realize that others are separate entities from themselves. Infants then begin to observe others' distress feelings and to share that distress. Many of such reactions end simply in empathy. But at other times infants may—often mistakenly—assume that they are the cause of the distress. This is because infants confuse causality with the contiguity of events: that is, true cause-and-effect sequences (a child pushes another who then cries) are not clearly distinguished from events that simply occur together (the child picks up a toy and the mother sneezes).[21] In Carolyn Zahn-Waxler's studies, toddlers have been observed apologizing to upset mothers and siblings in situations where the toddlers had done nothing wrong.[22]

By the end of the second year, advances in the child's conception of causality result in guilt becoming more clearly distinguished from empathy. The sense of personal blame becomes more firmly located in actions by the self resulting in harm to the other. Accordingly, guilt may be experienced when a child hits another child, breaks the other's toy, or causes a parent to become visibly sad. Martin Hoffman reports that he has observed children of two and three looking sad in such circumstances, and attempting to repair the harm by comforting the other.[23]

Several more advances in the guilt response occur during the period between early childhood and late adolescence. When children become cognizant of others' distinct inner feelings—around age three—they can become guilty about hurting those feelings (rather than only about hurting the other's body or possessions). Later, as the child understands more about the continued identity of others over time, the child develops the capacity to feel guilt over the effects that one's actions may have beyond the immediate situation. For example, an adolescent girl may worry that she has permanently hurt a boyfriend's self-esteem by her indifference.

Finally, there is the case of "existential guilt"—a late development that may affect people with acute social consciences.[24] Well-off people frequently feel some guilt over the gap between their own happy circumstances and the misfortunes of others. One example of this is the "survivor guilt" that has been reported by those who emerge unscathed from catastrophes like the Holocaust. Existential guilt may or may not reflect a sense of culpability over one's inactions, depending upon whether any actions were indeed realistic in the unfortunate circumstances. But in either case it can provide a continual spur towards benevolent social actions on behalf of life's victims—and it can also be a source of persistent, passive anguish if not effectively expressed.

Although shame and guilt have emotional tones that are radically different from that of empathy, their implications for children's morality are very much the same. Like empathy, shame and guilt have precursory roots in the earliest infant behavior. They derive from affective processes within the infant's natural constitution: they do not "come from nowhere," nor are they foisted upon an emotionally empty child by external social forces. Like empathy, both shame and guilt—and particularly guilt—change substantially throughout the course of development. They become inextricably intertwined with the child's cognitive growth and all that it encompasses. In the moral realm, this means that the child's cognitive awareness of others—their pain and joy, and their social perspectives—enhances and transforms the child's capacities to experience empathy, shame, and guilt.

The contemporary, post-Freudian emphasis on guilt's interpersonal nature also bears the same message for children's morality as our analysis of empathy and its development. Because these emotions are experienced in interpersonal settings, they are as much social as psychological in composition. This is to say that, at least in part, their existence is due to interpretations of events that are negotiated between people. An empathic response arises when one person accepts the reality of another's distress, and a guilt response arises when one person accepts responsibility for unjustly harming another. If there is doubt about the other's feelings, there can be no empathy; just as if one does not accept responsibility for the injury, there can be no guilt. Although the feelings have gut-level impact, their emergence depends on particular social interpretations.

Since these emotions arise and are played out in social contexts, it follows that they are most readily influenced and refined through social communication. This certainly has implications for our approach to children's moral education. We have seen above a glimpse of a group discussion method for fostering empathy and moral disgust in delinquent youth. This technique is effective precisely because it taps into deep emotions through real social experiences. Later chapters will describe the many ways in which powerful peer and adult relations in children's lives contribute naturally to children's acquisition of morality; and we shall explore other educational arrangements that make use of these relationships for spurring children to develop a still finer moral awareness.

Not all moral emotions are associated with one's own good or bad behavior. We may also experience strong feelings when we observe another person acting morally or immorally. In the case of moral behavior on the part of another, we feel admiration, awe, relief, or joy. In the case of another's immoral behavior, we feel contempt, fear, outrage, confusion, discouragement, or more generally, a persistent state of anxiety.

There is reason to believe that even very young children can have emotional reactions to moral events in which they do not directly participate. One source of such reactions lies in children's keen attention to their parents' behavior. Children respect the social competence of their parents and seek a similar mastery for themselves. An important part of such competence is knowing the rules of one's society and being able to regulate one's actions accordingly. Children are still ignorant of many social rules—and they are too impulsive to conform rigorously to the rules that they do know. But at the same time they are aware of the difficulty of these moral challenges. When they see their parents living up to complex standards, they glory in their parents' moral success. When they witness moral shortcomings on the part of a parent, children respond with anxiety and disappointment.

Jerome Kagan has traced the child's affective concern with standards as far back as the second year of life.[25] He has observed toddlers showing reactions of distress to toys that they discover in a damaged condition, even to the point of urgently seeking out their mothers to right the wrong. Kagan believes that these toddlers are demonstrating anxiety over a condition (broken toys) that they infer was brought about by actions deviating from moral standards. The toddlers seem to assume that the missing buttons on the toy dolls' dresses must have been torn off by someone and that the crayon marks on the soiled dolls' faces must have been mischievously put there. (These children, Kagan points out, do not become upset by benign alterations to toys, such as too many buttons on a doll's dress or an abnormally clean doll's face.) The anxiety that these toddlers express at the sight of inferred violations of standards is an early emotional response to secondhand moral events.

As the child's cognitive perspective broadens, it enlarges the sweep of the child's emotional response to observations of others' moral behavior. By early childhood there is a beginning awareness of justice and injustice as regards distribution of toys and other resources in the play group. Soon thereafter develops a sense of obligatory rules and other forms of social propriety. The range of moral concerns that are recognized by the end of childhood is as extensive as the child's social world itself, and includes interpersonal concerns about people that the child knows or has heard about as well as institutional concerns about family and societal life.

All of these burgeoning recognitions provide the child with incentives to assess and respond to other people's moral behavior. When the observed other is close to the self—as with a parent or a sibling—the response to a good deed might be pride, to a bad deed shame. When the observed other is more distant, the child might feel respect for the good deed, contempt or outrage at the bad deed. In each case, the emotion and its affiliated judgment present an opportunity to take a position on a moral value. Over time, particularly when the judgments are strongly felt, such positions will register deeply in the child's growing sense of right and wrong.

In sum, several important moral emotions—empathy, shame and guilt, and anxiety over other people's violations of standards—are present early in life and undergo continual developmental change throughout childhood and beyond. These emotions provide a natural base for the child's acquisition of moral values. As such, they both orient children toward moral events and motivate children to pay close attention to such events. These feelings provide the affective energy that motivate children's moral learning.

But moral emotions do not operate in a vacuum to build the child's moral awareness; nor are they sufficient in themselves to generate moral responsivity. They do not provide the "substance" of moral regulation—the actual rules, values, and standards of behavior that child must come to understand and act upon. Moral emotions are inextricably tied to the cognitive and social aspects of children's development. It is clear that the moral emotion can never exist alone: its fate is bound together with the other elements of the child's developing morality. When understood in this light, the moral emotions can offer us an invaluable point of entry into the child's moral awareness. Their hold on the child's attention is unparalleled. Such emotions also can have a marked impact on the child's tendency to recollect an experienced event.

The early moral emotions provide a ready-made affective structure upon which a child can build a set of deep and abiding moral concerns. The child, however, does not do so in isolation, but rather in the context of social experience and constructive social guidance. The social guidance that helps children refine their early moral emotions can come in many forms: as a conscious program of moral instruction offered by parents, teachers, and other adults; or as a spontaneous comment on one's conduct by friends, siblings, and other peers. In each case, children learn to know and interpret their own moral emotions in light of the moral reactions of others.

Sharing one's toys provides a common early childhood forum for experiencing moral reactions in a context of social guidance. As they give and receive objects, turns, and favors, children directly encounter others' (and their own) expectations of fairness and consideration. The outrage that a child feels when denied a fair share by a peer is as real as any moral emotion that will ever be felt. Children openly (and loudly) communicate such outrage to one another as well as to any supervising adults who may be at hand. As we shall see in the following chapter, this web of feeling and communication presents the child with an irreplaceable opportunity to learn about the importance and meaning of justice.

3

---•---

Learning about Justice
Through Sharing

There is no better example of children's morality than sharing, yet few adults recognize its true developmental significance. A child's sharing is an exercise in distributive justice, admittedly on a very small scale. But through the marvel of human development, small-scale exercises tend one day to become activities of the gravest import. And there is no graver human concern than one of distributive justice. Many of humanity's great battles, military as well as political, have been waged by people contending for their fair share of some treasured commodity.

How should the world's resources be allocated among all the people who lay claim to them? What does it mean to "deserve" something? How should we balance the rights of someone who has earned something against the rights of someone who may need it more? These are problems of distributive justice on a grand scale; and, despite centuries of philosophical and economic debate, they are problems that have eluded a definitive resolution (or, judging from the amount of conflict in the world today, even a barely satisfactory one). The most sophisticated legal theorists of our time still search for sounder methods of adjudicating intricately complex claims over land, water, food, minerals, money, and every other form of wealth.

Conflicts of distributive justice in adult life can be complex to the point of intractability, but their basic principles are similar to ones that young children wrestle with almost daily. Sharing is a regular practice in every child's life, beginning as soon as the child interacts with other children—often during the first year of life. This sets sharing apart from the many moral concerns (for example, the concern for protecting human life) that are discovered only as the growing child acquires the experience and responsibilities of social maturity.

31

Because sharing has such an early and enduring significance, understanding its origins will provide us with a key to children's morality. Understanding children's sharing means knowing why children do it in the first place as well as when (and under what conditions) they are most likely to do it or refuse to do it. It also means knowing how children's sharing changes during the course of development. This requires knowing children's intellectual rationales for their sharing decisions and how these rationales change with age; and it also requires knowing the less conscious psychological processes that influence children's sharing conduct. In many ways these are the archtypical questions of moral development.

Parents encourage children to share as a way of being "nice" to others, but this is not the only reason that children do it. Sharing is often the price of admission to an enjoyable social activity. A child with a toy can entice another child into playing games by offering to share the toy. The toy can be the bait that lures the other child into a social engagement. Although this may sound like a ploy that is too clever or too manipulative for a young child to use, in fact very young children spontaneously use objects in exactly this manner. Observations have shown that a child's first peer engagements are almost invariably object-centered.[1] During infancy, children discover by chance that other infants share an interest in toys and that joint play with the same toy is more fun and more interesting than solitary play. It does not take the child long to turn this discovery into an active strategy for initiating peer engagements.

In addition, the ritual of sharing is itself pleasurable for young children. Piaget long ago showed that children's early play and games are largely based on rituals.[2] Sharing is one of the playful rituals of childhood that young children spontaneously discover and enjoy. They especially delight in the symmetry and predictability of turn-taking. "Taking turns" on a swing set provides a back-and-forth social rhythm that can be as much fun for children as the back-and-forth physical rhythm that they get on the very same swing set.

This is not to say that sharing is *always* fun for the child. To the contrary, conflicts over toys and objects far outnumber episodes of spontaneous sharing, at least in the first few years of life.[3] Many is the time that a child would rather forego the social joy of sharing the swing in favor of the physical joy of staying on it. Children are not selfless saints, nor are they born with behavior-determining genes for altruism, despite the extravagant claims of certain socio-biologists.[4] Consistent generosity, when it exists in human affairs, comes only as a product of long-term moral development. In early childhood, acts of sharing are irregular, erratic, and usually more bound to the needs of the self than those of the other. Still, such acts are performed, and often voluntarily because they are themselves a source of fun for the child.

Occasionally, children also do share for reasons that can be called genuinely altruistic. We saw in the last chapter how the child's capacity for empathy begins early in life and grows continually throughout the subsequent years. Empathy provides a compelling motive for altruistic acts like sharing. A child witnessing another child in distress sometimes will experience the other's sorrow and react by offering the other a toy as a means of comfort. Children often give away portions of their food and candy in order to experience jointly the empathic pleasure of eating with a friend. They also can give generously to one another on birthdays and other special occasions.

In addition to parental cajoling and positive affective incentives, there are also negative peer pressures on children to share. The impending risk of conflict always looms over children who act stingy and "hog" all the desired resources. Fighting over toys begins as soon as children play with other children. As noted above, in toddler play groups, struggles over toys are the most frequent type of encounter. Clearly such conflict provides children with an early pragmatic reason for learning to share.

Understanding why children share means not only explaining their behavior from the outside but also entering into the child's own meaning for the sharing act. Because of sharing's central importance for children's morality, an "internal view" of sharing can provide us with a window on the child's burgeoning moral perspective. The first questions we must ask are: Why do children think it is important to share? What do they know and believe about issues of fairness and resource distribution in general?

Along with these questions about why children think they share go many related questions about how their standards of fairness influence their actual behavior. What considerations do children take into account when deciding how (and whether) to share their own belongings with others? Do children split up toys and food differently with different friends or acquaintances, and do they also do so differently as conditions change? What about their views on distributive justice in the world at large, beyond the familiar circles of their own friends and possessions? Is there variation between individual children in the tendency to share? Do a child's standards of fairness change as the child grows older; and if so, do such changes accompany new forms of moral conduct?

Our knowledge of children's earliest conceptions of fairness is inferential, because infants and toddlers do not have the verbal skills to answer extended queries about why they share. We must rely instead on observations of children's social behavior, a far less direct way of arriving at the ideas behind their acts. The most that we can say from such observations is that by the end of infancy, the child begins to hold an *expectation* that sharing will occur in some circumstances. This expectation is most apparent when children take turns while playing with an object. When in control of the object, a child in her second year often will spontaneously offer another child (or a parent) a turn. When not in control of the object, the same child will wait for, and eventually demand, her own turn.

The same behavior can be observed with food, particularly if the food is attractive and divisible. Children in the second year of life show expectations that pieces of candy may be divided, ice cream cones may be licked, and cookies may be bitten into. These expectations lead to pointed requests if the child is a potential recipient; and (often, though not always) they lead to offers if the child is fortunate enough to be on the donating end.

This does not mean that infants or toddlers consider sharing to be an *obligation* in the moral sense, except insofar as it may comply with parental or other adult demands. Indeed, when not in the immediate presence of an authority figure, very young children's sharing is erratic and somewhat whimsical in nature. As noted above, most turn-taking and "dividing up" between children in the first three years of life is playful, done purely out of enjoyment. Judging from this, it appears that very young children view sharing as a voluntary and irregular part of social life, unless of course it is demanded by an authority figure who is present. Other acts of sharing may be imitative, strictly in emulation of adults and older siblings. In none of these cases does there appear to be an inner norm or ethic that justifies sharing on its own behalf.

Do very young children *ever* believe that sharing is something that one *should* do, for intrinsic reasons of morality beyond play and imitation? A two- or three-year-old's empathic awareness of another's feelings certainly provides the child with one moral incentive to share, as well as a moral rationale with which to justify sharing. Further, when parents urge children to share with one another, they often invoke the feelings of the child's playmates as a reason: "Ginny will feel sad if you don't give her some," or "Think how happy your little brother will be if you let him have a turn with your new toy." This kind of reasoned urging communicates to children a cultural norm of kindness that supports the child's natural feelings of empathy.

We may conclude, therefore, that empathy provides children with their first intrinsically moral sense of obligation to share. *Most* early sharing during the first three years of life is done for nonempathic reasons: for the fun of the social play ritual, from unquestioning deference to an authority figure's demands, or out of mere imitation. But this does not reduce the importance of the initial empathy-driven act, since developmentally it is the first step towards the major reasoning and behavioral systems soon to follow.

It is around the child's fourth year that the combination of natural empathic awareness and reasoned adult encouragement leads the child to develop a firm sense of obligation to share with others. This obligation compels the child to share even under conditions where the child may not see this as the best way to have fun. The advent of this perspective makes the child a more reliable and consistent sharer, even in the absence of authority figures. This is still not to say that the four-year-old child is a selfless saint. Children now believe that they should share, but not necessarily that they should be equally as generous to others as to the self. Nor do their actions always live up to their beliefs, particularly when the object of contention is highly desirable. But what is crucial developmentally is that there is now an internal belief in sharing as an obligatory part of any social relationship; and moreover that this is a question of right and wrong.

By the age of four or five, children can be interviewed about their views on moral standards like sharing and fairness. In order to probe a young child's understanding of fairness, researchers use actual objects to base their questioning on. For example, in the 1950s a Turkish psychologist named Rafia Ugerel-Semin did a pioneering study of children's sharing by providing children with nuts to divide between themselves and a peer.[5] The children were then asked to explain why they shared the nuts with the other child. Other researchers following Ugerel-Semin's lead have used poker chips, toys, candy, and pennies for similar purposes.

In addition to such questions and props, investigators have explored children's prosocial reasoning with techniques ranging from naturalistic observation to laboratory experimentation. Nancy Eisenberg and her colleagues recorded preschool children's spontaneous acts of sharing and helping.[6] They then asked the children to express their own reasons for these "real life" prosocial acts.

In another approach, Daniel Bar-Tal and his colleagues artificially stimulated much the same type of behavior.[7] In this experiment, children were given an opportunity to share some candy they had won with a child who did not win any. Bar-Tal set up experimental conditions in which the first child (a) was simply left alone with the second child, (b) was told by an adult that some children share their winnings, (c) was ordered to share by the adult, or (d) was offered an additional reward to share. Bar-Tal recorded the sharing decisions of children in each of these conditions, and then asked all of the children to provide reasons for their behavior.

Virtually all the techniques cited above have found four-year-olds already in possession of active, flourishing conceptions of fairness. Most children at this age have firmly internalized the standard of sharing. They know that they have an obligation to share at least some part of their possessions with others on occasion. This does not mean that they always do so (as any parent can attest), but rather that they believe it is something that they ought to do in many circumstances.

What is the child's own rationale for this belief? During the preschool years, children express a number of contending justifications for the standard of sharing. The first and most common reason for sharing is provided by the *empathic* rationale, now offered more consistently than when the child was younger. A four-year-old will often say that he shares because "it makes the other kid happy," or because "when I don't my friend gets sad and feels like crying." This type of reasoning derives directly from the child's well-developed affective capacity for empathic responding and indirectly from the reasons that parents often give to accompany their demands that children share.

Some reasons for sharing stated by four-year-olds are less other-oriented. Four-year-olds commonly express *pragmatic* concerns that, they say, lead them to share with others. Among these are their desires to avoid punishment and to be rewarded. A four-year-old may say that she shares because the consequences of not sharing are unpleasant. An adult may disapprove, or a playmate may become angry. Conversely, generosity sometimes brings rewards: a sharing act may be rewarded by a parent or may be reciprocated by a peer. Preschoolers are aware of such pragmatic contingencies, and take them as good reasons to be fair with their friends.

There are many preschool notions about fairness that may not strike us as very fair by adult standards. These notions generally are of the *egoistic* variety, and often favor the self at the expense of certain others. One such notion is the belief that sharing is right whenever I want to do it—that is, when it is fun to do, or when I am with someone that I am especially fond of. Otherwise it is not so necessary. Related to this is the notion that fairness is fine among persons with whom one identifies, but need not extend beyond one's chosen circle of associates. Preschoolers sometimes draw boundaries around their gender groups in a predictable way: boys blatantly favor boys, and girls likewise favor girls.

Children's responses to the stories and questions of the kind quoted above provide illustrations of the preschooler's many-faceted ideas about fairness. Sometimes these ideas seem surprisingly trenchant; other times they seem contradictory and self-serving. Take the following three examples, from a task in which children were asked if they would share any poker chips with an imaginary friend. The children in these examples are all four years old.

1. (Gives five chips to the friend, keeps four to herself.) Why did you give these to your friend? *Because I like her.* What if you just kept them for yourself? *Then she would go home crying and I won't have anyone to play with.*

2. (Gives three to himself, three to the friend, keeps three aside.) Why did you give these to your friend? *Because I like to share my things.* Why is that? *Because if I want him to let me play with his, I have to give him some of mine.* What if you just keep these all for yourself? *Then he may say to me, "Too bad, you never give me anything, why should I?"*

3. (Keeps seven chips, including all the blues, for herself, and gives her friend "Jenny" two white ones.) You would keep all the blues

for yourself? *Yes, because I like blue. And then I'd play with them.* Let's pretend Jenny said, "I like blue." Would you give her any blue? *Never, because I have a blue dress at home.* So you wouldn't give her any blue at all. Is it fair to do it this way? *Ah ha, I've got it. I'd give her two of the white—I'd give her those because she's younger than me, and I get four because I'm four.*

We can see in these three examples the range of concerns—from the caring to the calculating—that characterizes children's early understanding of sharing and fairness. The first child is aware of the distress that her refusing to share would create in a friend. She also knows that such distress could have adverse consequences for her playtime fun. This blend of empathy and pragmatism, in her view, justifies her generosity.

The second child is also pragmatic in his rationale for fairness. He understands the reciprocal nature of social interaction, and explains his sharing decision accordingly. For this child, the point of sharing is that people tend to treat you in kind. This is not quite the Golden Rule yet, but it is certainly a form of understanding that is precursory to it. The boy's appraisal of sharing's (and not sharing's) reciprocal consequences is astute and realistic.

The third child knows that it is important to share yet does not care to give away the most valued objects. Her reasoning weaves a convoluted web of egoistic justifications in support of her choice. But these justifications also include some objective-seeming elements (her belongings, her age—in other words, criteria that exist in reality, beyond the subject's internal wishes). The fact that she feels compelled to offer justifications that at least *appear* objective indicates that this young girl has firmly internalized the sharing standard. She bends considerations of fairness to her own purposes, but she does not wholly ignore them. If her behavior is self-serving, her justifications at least are beginning to be guided by a felt sense of obligation to distribute goods fairly.

The three children quoted above demonstrate the progress that children normally have achieved in understanding fairness by the end of the preschool years. First, and most importantly, they generally believe that sharing is an obligatory act. Further, they are aware of some moral reasons that justify this obligation. The primary moral reason invoked at this age is empathy, but there are also inklings of other moral justifications that will become more fully developed later.

For example, as the second child quoted above demonstrates, preschool children can express a preliminary form of tit-for-tat reciprocity as a reason for sharing; and, as the third child demonstrates, preschoolers sometimes try to cite objective criteria as grounds for their distributive justice decisions. In the final analysis, these grounds are not truly objective but rather are transparently derived from the preschooler's wishes; just as the preschooler's sense of reciprocity does not constitute a moral duty but rather a pragmatic means of getting one's way. Still, despite their shortcomings, these early notions of justice directly set the stage for the giant strides about to be made in the next few years.

By the beginning of the elementary school years, children begin to express more genuinely objective notions of fairness with some regularity. These further notions include basic categories of justice that have been used throughout human history to distribute goods and to resolve conflicts. Among these ancient categories are the principles of *equality, merit,* and *benevolence.*

Equality at its core means ensuring that everyone is treated the same. Of course there are a number of elaborate ways of attempting this, such as equal opportunity, affirmative action, equal rights, and so on; but for a child, equality means concretely identical acts of distribution. Merit, on the other hand, means giving extra rewards for hard work, for a talented performance, or for some other laudatory activity. Benevolence means giving special consideration for those in a condition of disadvantage (like the needy or the handicapped). Through such principles children establish objective criteria for reaching decisions about what is fair.

Among most elementary school children, equality is the first of these principles to be used regularly. It is common to hear six-year-olds use the word "fair" synonymously with the words "equal" or "same." Although children in the early grades sometimes have a sense of equal opportunity (as in giving everyone a fair chance to win a contest), more commonly they are concerned simply with equal shares. As suggested above, the notion of "equalizing" through *unequal* treatment (as in giving an extra boost to those who are starting from behind as a gesture towards equal opportunity) is not common at this age.

Soon after children begin thinking of fairness in terms of equality, merit- or benevolence-based considerations begin to become apparent to them. Social scientists have called these considerations of merit and benevolence "principles of equity." In this usage, equity means special treatment in favor of persons who "deserve" it. Deciding who deserves equity is, of course, a subjective process, because there are many grounds for claiming it. In our culture, merit is probably the most common ground for such claims. Another common claim is disadvantage; and, related to this, past grievances that require redressing. Others include investment, kinship, and inheritance. These claims vie with one another in every probate court case and in practically every political debate.

Studies have shown that children develop an appreciation of equity within a year or two after they have fully understood the importance of equality for fairness. By mid-to-late elementary school, children can draw on a number of considerations in resolving a problem in justice. They can take into account claims of hard work, poverty, talent (or its lack), investment, and simple equality. They can weight such claims against each other in order to reach a decision. Towards the end of this period, children even can juggle several competing claims at once, devising compromise solutions in which each claim is given some recognition.

For elementary school aged children, researchers have used story problems as a means of probing children's reasoning about sharing and fairness. Children are told a story and then asked to respond with choices about how the story's problem is best resolved. The children's choices, and their reasons for their choices, provide us with good indicators of their thinking about fairness. One story problem that has been widely used with elementary-aged children goes as follows. The child is shown pictures of several children and a schoolteacher, then told:

All these boys and girls are in the same class together (pictures of story characters are shown). One day their teacher let them spend the whole afternoon making paintings and crayon drawings. The teacher thought that these pictures were so good that the class could sell them at the school fair. The pictures were all sold, and together the class made a whole lot of money. The children gathered the next day and tried to decide how to give out the money.[8]

The child is then asked questions about the story:

What do you think they should do with the money? Why?

Kathy said the kids in the class who made the best pictures should get the most money. What do you think?

There were kids who were lazy and spent their time fooling around while the others were drawing pictures. What about them?

Melissa says the girls should get more, and Danny says the boys should get more. What do you think?

Someone said that the kids who come from poor families should get more. What do you think?

Someone said that the teacher should get a lot because it was her idea to do the pictures in the first place. Should she?

Someone said that everyone should get the same amount, no matter what. Do you agree?

Can you take this [play money] and show us the very best way to give out the money?

The following responses to the dilemma from children six to twelve years old illustrate the development of school-age children's abilities to think about fairness. The first child considers only equality. The other children introduce a number of "equity" concerns, beginning with the strictly meritorian claims advanced by the second child. Note the increasingly intricate verbal juggling performed by the last two children. They weigh, sift through, and discard justice claims much as a judge weighs the stated positions and grievances of judicial protagonists.

1. Do you think anyone should get any more than anyone else? *No, because it's not fair. Somebody has thirty-five cents and somebody has one penny. That's not fair. . . .* George said that he thought the ones who made the best stuff should get the most money. *The best person who made the best stuff is not polite, because you should make them have the same— give everything the same. The same, because it's not polite when you give people the most and they* [the rest of the people] *don't have one. It's fair to the other children that they have to get it too.*

2. *Well, if she made more things, she'd get more money.* What if she didn't? *If she didn't want to make anything, then she wouldn't get as much as all of these kids.* Well, what about the poor kid here, who doesn't have any money to begin with? *Well, the poor kid should make some stuff, then he'd get more.* What about the lazy kid? *Well, he shouldn't get as much if he didn't work as much, if he didn't do his work.*

3. What if Rebecca made more stuff? Should she get more money?

Oh, about seven more pennies. It depends on what she made—if she made some-thing easy or hard. What if she made something hard? *About ten cents more.* What about Peter, who made the best stuff? *Well, maybe he should. But since she [Rebecca] made more, she may have some good ones [too], so then maybe he can get around five cents more.* What about Billy, who doesn't get any allowance? *He should only get about three cents more, because—if he got a lot more, he might even have more than anybody adding up their allowance.* What about these others? *No, because they don't have such a big reason.*

4. Should the kids who were most cooperative get bigger shares? *No! Because that really doesn't make much sense. They are not in a contest about attitude and how you share with other people. They don't care about that. They just want to have people do good stuff.* How about giving bigger shares to the poor kids? *No. They don't care if they are poor or not. Well, we might feel a little sorry for them. But they don't care about that. They just want the ones who did the best to get the most money.* And why is that? *I just said, that way they'll all try to do better next time.*[9]

From these examples we can see how children in the elementary school years weigh equality, merit, need, and other social concerns in reaching decisions about fairness. In addition, empathic con-cerns for another's feelings, and pragmatic concerns about the con-sequences of not sharing both continue to weigh heavily, just as they did in the preschool years.

Missing from the concerns that have been identified as guiding children's sharing is one that we adults might expect to be the most influential of all: the urge to obey the commands of adult authority figures. This omission is surprising, because it is certainly true that children generally do feel an obligation to obey their parents and teachers. It is also true that parents and teachers constantly insist that children share. And in fact, from time to time a child in the preschool or elementary school years may say that he shares with friends because some authority figure told him to. But this is rare. In general, authority-obeying plays only a minor role in the ratio-nales that children express to justify their acts of sharing and fair-ness.

Surprising though the relatively small influence of authority on sharing may seem, study after study has borne it out. For example, when Nancy Eisenberg obtained children's explanations for their own real life prosocial acts, they offered mostly empathic and pragmatic reasons for their spontaneous acts of sharing.[10] Not one of Eisenberg's children referred to the dictates of authority.

Similarly, investigators using the school fair dilemma almost never find children basing their fairness decisions upon what a parent or teacher would say.[11] Researchers using experimental techniques consistently report the same.[12] Neither authoritarian influences nor concerns about the rules and expectations of adult society have much effect on children's prosocial reasoning. Even when such authoritarian or normative concerns emerge in a child's prosocial reasoning on a rare occasion, they are overshadowed by the far more common concerns of empathy and justice.

These findings are counterintuitive, largely because we adults often believe that children's "good" behavior is a product of our own ministrations to them. This belief is manifest in the way we attribute responsibility for children's deeds and misdeeds: for example, it is typical for parents to assume credit or blame for their child's character, in their own eyes as well as in the eyes of others.

Parental advice and prodding certainly help foster standards of sharing. But the give and take of peer requests, arguments, conflicts, and acts of generosity provide the most immediate spur. Parents may set examples that their children carry with them into the peer fray. A parent may offer counsel that proves critical at strategic points in the child's experimentation with sharing solutions. But parents cannot be present during all of their children's peer encounters. The day-to-day construction of fairness standards in social life must be done by children in collaboration with one another.

In their daily exchanges of toys and favors, children communicate a world of expectations to one another. They pressure one another to act fairly and, in the process, invent a large (often ingenious) variety of new claims to justice. These negotiations encourage children to think in increasingly sophisticated ways about what is fair. Over the course of many years and many thousands of encounters, the child's understanding of justice deepens.

The natural learning encounters that children provide for one another through peer interchange are effective precisely because they contain all the immediacy, complexity, and ambiguity of real life. Consider the following episode, recorded in a Worcester pizza parlor by one of my Clark University graduate students. It would be difficult, if not impossible, for we as adults to structure for chil-

dren as rich a tutorial in distributive justice. Seven children, all
wearing hockey uniforms, walked into the pizza parlor to order
one large cheese pizza. The incident began when the waiter deliv-
ered the pizza.

WAITER: OK kids, here's your pizza. [The children then each
took one piece].

CHILD 1: Hey, there's eight pieces here. What about the extra
piece?

CHILD 2: The guy who's the oldest should get it. How old are
you?

CHILD 1: Nine.

CHILD 3: I'm nine and a quarter.

CHILD 1: My birthday's coming up this summer. I'm—I'll be ten
in one, two months.

CHILD 2 (to Child 4): How old are you?

CHILD 4: Eleven, and I'll be twelve next month.

CHILD 2: Well, I'm twelve, so I'll get the extra piece.

CHILD 1: What about giving it to the one with the small piece?

CHILD 4: Well who's got the smallest piece?

CHILD 1: I've got the smallest piece—look at it!

CHILD 2: C'mon, let's cut it. The oldest kid will get one piece
and the kid with the smallest piece will get one piece.

CHILD 3: I bet I can name everybody's names here. You're
Michael, you're Louie, you're Johnie.

CHILD 2: You're Joey, you're Louie . . . [names all the other
children].

CHILD 4: [Names all of the others' names faster than Child 2 or
3].

CHILD 5: Hey, can we get some water here? Who's gonna play
hockey tomorrow?

CHILD 3: I am, I am. [Jumps up and moves over to the pizza tray,
which still has the extra piece on it. Begins picking cheese off
the top. Child 1 and Child 2 gather around, each taking
chunks of the extra piece, with Child 3 getting the lion's
share.]

CHILD 6: Who's the biggest eater here? Who's the piggiest?

CHILD 2: I can eat seven pieces of pizza, but I gotta give one to my mother.

CHILD 6: No, no. Who's the biggest eater of us all?

CHILD 4: Joey [Child 3] is.

CHILD 1: Yeah, Joey is.

CHILD 3: Yeah, I can eat two whole pizzas myself.

CHILD 1: Two whole pizzas.

CHILD 6: Yeah, you're the biggest pig all right.

Episodes like this one, common in every child's life, offer ready-made instruction about the role of fairness in resolving conflicting human interests. In this situation, the group presence forced each individual child to refrain from unadorned assertions of self-interest. Rather than simply grabbing for the extra piece, the children initially cast about for a principle that could justify a fair distribution. Before the debate ended, the group had discussed giving the extra piece to the oldest child and to the child with the smallest piece—ideas that, not coincidentally, were introduced by the two children with claims to these two criteria. The episode was finally resolved not through a just decision but by grabbing. But even here there was some group feedback that could be heard as a message about fairness (or its absence): Child 6, acting as a kind of Greek chorus, commented acidly about Child 3's greedy behavior.

Because such incidents are not accompanied by carefully directed adult messages, they are by no means complete guides to moral behavior. Such incidents contain many elements that have more to do with self-serving behavior than with justice; and many other elements that pose for the child a confusing blend of the two. In the above example, it is clear that many Machiavellian strategies were at play in this childhood social conflict; and, in terms of the final pizza distribution, these strategies prevailed. But it is also clear that other, more subtle, social rewards were at stake, including esteem in the eyes of other group members. Ultimately, adult guidance can help a child sort out some of these tangled issues, clarifying for the child the true purpose and rewards of justice. But as a means of impressing upon the child the overall importance of these concerns, nothing can substitute for the child's actual confrontations in real life peer engagements.

Through such engagements and the accompanying guidance of advising adults, children develop a rich understanding of fairness during the first decade of life. But how well does this understanding translate into just action? Do children merely learn to talk about how important it is to be fair? Or do they, in addition, actually share the valued things in their lives with one another? Do their beliefs about fairness have anything to do with how they actually distribute rewards between people with conflicting claims to the rewards?

The relation between judgment and conduct is one of the central issues in the study of moral development, and it is also one of the most difficult and complex. There are no simple answers to the question of whether moral ideas lead to moral action. It is not possible, for example, to predict from a person's moral views how the person will behave in a particular situation. Virtually all social science studies based on such direct predictions have fallen flat. Perhaps the best known of such cases was Hartshorne and May's epic attempt, described in Chapter 1. But there have been many others, all with the same generally disappointing results.[13] No matter how much we know about a person's moral beliefs, we cannot predict with any certainty the person's every act across the range of life's specific social circumstances.

In large part, as Hartshorne and May themselves wrote, this is because a specific social context is likely to lead someone to act in a certain way, regardless of that individual's moral beliefs. Most people, for example, would tell a lie to save a life in a death-threatening situation, whatever their views on honesty. The situation has its own demands, and these demands may be so strong that they obliterate the differences between people's moral beliefs.

Nevertheless, moral judgment does make a difference for moral conduct. But it does not operate in a vacuum. It shares its influence with many social-contextual factors that also play some role, though not the only role, in determining a person's behavior.

In fact, a person's understanding of moral issues can give us some important clues about how the person will approach similar problems as they arise in real life. Even though this may not enable us to know exactly what the person will do in all possible conditions, it will help us make informed guesses about the person's tendencies towards moral action. We may expect, for example, that a person who believes strongly in equal sharing will, over a long course of events, tend to distribute goods more evenly than one who believes strongly in preferential treatment for merit or need. Some special conditions will no doubt confound this expectation from time to time. As we know more about the nature of such conditions and how they affect the person's behavior, our predictions will become even sharper.

Trends in children's sharing behavior, therefore, may be linked to trends in their understanding of fairness, but these links sometimes will be weakened by particular circumstances. One example of this was reported by William Froming and his colleagues.[14] Froming examined children's willingness to donate their candy to other children who had none. Most children in his age sample (six to eight years) readily express such willingness. But not all actually do so. Froming believed that children who firmly understood other people's points of view would be more likely to donate candy than those who had a shaky understanding, because the former have greater empathic capacities. He did in fact find this, but only in conditions where an adult was present to monitor the children's behavior. Thus only the *combination* of advanced empathic understanding and adult presence predicted sharing. Understanding and action were linked in conditions where action was further prodded by an external influence.

Research comparing children's reasoning on story problems to their behavior in real life situations has uncovered similar patterns. For example, children who understood and expressed a preference for merit-based solutions on the school fair dilemma also showed such preference in an experimental situation designed to emulate this hypothetical story in real life.[15] But they did so most markedly when *they themselves* had the strongest claim to preferred treatment—such as, for example, when they had done the best job. Otherwise they tended more towards equal solutions. Self-interest was clearly a mitigating factor in children's actual attempts to be fair. As a further indication of self-interest's lure, the presence of real candy bars as the disputed resource in this situation acted as a powerful incentive for children to devise solutions favoring themselves. A control group given cardboard imitations to distribute acted two or three times more generously than the children who were asked to distribute the real thing.

But all this should not be interpreted to mean that self-interest was the only dominant factor and that the child's understanding of fairness played no role. The meritorian solutions may have been self-favoring, but not so much so as the solutions of the very young children who understood neither equality nor merit. These children often boldly attempted to give themselves the lion's share on the basis of egoistic claims such as the simple wishes of self. Or they referred to "objective" (but transparently self-identifying) claims such as their size or gender (for example, "I should get all these because I'm big," or "We two girls would like these many"). The younger children's decisions, therefore, were consistent with their own, largely self-serving, beliefs about distributive justice.

In contrast to the younger children, the older children favored themselves with meritorian solutions rather than blatant assertions of desire or the self-oriented use of "objective" criteria such as their age or gender. These meritorian solutions, though certainly some-what biased, were nevertheless more fair to others than the solu-tions of the younger children. For one thing, the meritorian solu-tions led to relatively modest claims rather than to wholesale demands for the lion's share. Further, the older children applied their meritorian solutions not only to themselves but also in equal proportions to other children with similar merit claims. There was, therefore, some consistency in their positions regarding fairness. Finally, these children also were careful to award children with less meritorious performances some reasonable share. Thus it seems that, although understanding fairness does not eradicate self-interest, it does temper it and make it increasingly enlightened.

In line with this general conclusion, a concordance of studies has shown that children show a greater tendency to share and co-operate with one another as their moral understanding develops.[16] Although young children occasionally perform a spontaneous pro-social act, such activity is relatively rare and undependabile. Its erratic quality is very much in keeping with the child's reasoning about fairness in the preschool years. With the advent of notions of equality, merit, and benevolence in the elementary school years, the child's behavior becomes more consistent, more responsible, and indeed more fair.

Observational evidence for this change has been available since the beginning of child psychology as a scientific discipline. In one of the psychology's first investigations of natural childhood life, Lois Murphy observed that spontaneous sharing occurs on occa-sion, but is far from the norm by the time of nursery school.[17] In fact, she reported that young children's peer relations reveal a se-vere imbalance of antisocial over prosocial behavior. In Murphy's data on preschool-age children, aggressive and selfish interactions outnumber sharing, helping, and "kind" interactions by a ratio of eight to one. Murphy's observations were done in the 1930s in

Minnesota, but they are hardly out of date: a 1981 California study by Wanda Bronson shows much the same early scarcity of sharing relative to fighting and grabbing in very young children.[18]

With age and developing moral values, children become increasingly generous and helpful in their everyday behavior. Sharing becomes a dominant characteristic of the child's peer relations rather than just an occasional act. This change goes hand in hand with other changes that increase the stability and cooperativeness of children's peer relations over time.

Children's sharing, as we have seen, arises as a natural response to common social experiences. The social experiences can be found anywhere that children have friends and playthings, and the natural responses that we have identified may be universal as well. Specifically, we can point to the following familiar social and emotional sources of children's sharing:

1. The child's initial tendency to approach playmates through a common interest in toys and other objects.

2. The pleasure derived through the symmetrical rhythm of turn-taking with toys and other objects.

3. The insistence of peers and parents that objects be divided and shared when possible.

4. The child's natural empathic response to another child who may desire a turn or a share, bolstered by the adult's reasoned message that the other child will be unhappy in the absence of sharing.

5. The child's pragmatic desires to stay in the good graces of a playmate out of an expectation that the playmate will reciprocate.

These common occurrences engender sharing, and sharing in turn engenders the child's first concerns over distributive justice and fairness. While morality is thus deeply rooted in children's early social and emotional lives, it does not remain frozen at this early point. As we have seen, there is rapid development in both sharing and morality in general throughout the childhood years. Children's understanding of fairness becomes increasingly elaborate as notions like equality, merit, benevolence, and compromise are established. With this conceptual elaboration comes a greater consistency and generosity in children's sharing behavior. While self-interest is never eradicated, it increasingly is placed in the perspective of others' needs and claims to justice.

Children's morality, therefore, is as much a story of developmental change as of early natural inclinations. Without developmental change a child would remain at best erratic and unpredictable in her urges to act morally. This is why I reject the nativist theories that are currently in vogue. Of course it is equally wrong to say that without development we would have a "blank slate" of a child without any natural moral predispositions at all, which is why I reject wholly environmentalist or social-cultural positions on children's morality. The truth is less simple and more encompassing than any of these extreme positions: it is the process of development that transforms the child's nascent prosocial orientation into a full-fledged moral perspective, replete with complex systems of judgment and action.

What is this "process of development" that accounts for such a major moral transformation? If we can provide a good answer to this question we are well on our way towards understanding how to intervene positively and effectively in spurring children's moral growth. We know that this developmental transformation starts early and continues throughout the childhood years, and that it relies on many key experiences and social influences. The child encounters some of these key experiences and influences through relations with adults, others through relations with peers; some in the family, others with friends and acquaintances. Throughout it all, the child actively interprets the events and reconciles them in her own way. Such interpretations provide a framework for the child's constantly expanding moral awareness. The child's experiences, social influences, and natural inclinations provide the bricks and mortar that turn this moral awareness into moral character.

4

Parental Authority and the Rules of the Family

A family is a small social system; and, like any social system, families have rules of conduct. In many cases, family rules are similar to those of society at large, except that family rules are not written into any formal legal code. Families, like societies at large, have prohibitions against disorder, dishonesty, theft, violence, and incest. Acts of cruelty and hostility breach familial as well as societal regulations. In both family and society, such offenses are discouraged through sanctions like disapproval and punishment.

For children in a family, parents act as the chief enforcers of social regulation. Parents obviously have a great deal of power over children, particularly when the children are young: not only do parents possess the advantages of strength, size, and competence over children, but they also are needed by their children for protection and nurturance. Consequently, parents are in a good position to uphold family rules and to administer sanctions for violations of these rules.

Because family rules often overlap with society's rules, parental enforcements present a double message to children: this is prohibited here and this is wrong in general. In this way, the child's first encounter with societal regulations is likely to occur in the home. A parent's command to stop hitting little sister communicates a sanction against violence, a sanction that the child soon realizes applies well beyond the scope of the family.

For this reason, the parent (or the parent substitute) has a critical and irreplaceable role in the child's moral development. It is the parent who first introduces the child to the laws and logic of the social order. In addition to informing children about sanctions within and beyond the family, this means enforcing these sanctions and communicating to the child their social purpose.

51

But introducing children to the social order means more than just getting them to obey certain rules. It also means inculcating in children an abiding respect for social order itself. All social systems have principles of hierarchy and regulation that are essential for the systems' functioning as well as their cohesion. If a social system is to work well, these principles must be known, respected, and consistently implemented. Roles and responsibilities must be distributed and members of the social system must cooperate to accept their own allotted positions. This means that authority must be assumed by some and deferred to by others. These roles may be renegotiated over time. Nevertheless, barring a revolution, there must be some shared willingness to follow, at least for a time, the roles and regulations prescribed by the present social order.

Parents' authority and the shared rules of conduct maintained by their authority are essential both for the family's social functioning and for the child's growing moral awareness. The child's respect for this authority is the single most important moral legacy that comes out of the child's relations with the parent. (Other legacies—such as a belief in justice and other moral values—are also crucial, but they are not as much confined to the domain of parental influence). The child's respect for parental authority sets the direction for civilized participation in the social order when the child later begins assuming the rights and responsibilities of full citizenship.

Although parents have at their disposal the power to punish, force is by no means a parent's only means of getting children to respect authority or to comply with social rules. The closely affectionate relationship that most parents enjoy with their children normally induces an inclination to cooperate. Studies by Mary Ainsworth and her colleagues show that young children securely attached to their parents are the ones most likely to comply with family rules.[1] These children actively seek and accept the adult's guidance. In this sense, secure children obey voluntarily from "within" the relationship, rather than out of coercion or fear.

Aside from punishment and love, parents induce good behavior in their children through such strategies as appeals to reason, cajoling, and outright bribery. As an example with dietary rather than moral significance, many parents customarily will hold their children's dessert in ransom until the children have downed at least a token portion of leafy green vegetable. Incentives for moral behavior within the family are structued in much the same way—as are those in the world outside.

The family, then, is the first context for learning society's rules and the obligation to obey. Consequently, it is the primary agent of "socialization" during the child's early years. But not all families socialize children in the same way. There is great variation from one family to the next in how children are treated, raised, and communicated with, as well as in how they are induced to follow social rules. Such variation accounts for important differences between children in their later propensities towards moral and not-so-moral behavior.

Through conversations, confrontations, and other exchanges with parents and siblings, children at an early age discover the social rules implicit in family life. Judy Dunn and her colleagues have observed toddlers in some of their first introductions to family rules.[2] Two of Dunn's examples are as follows:

1. Child (16 months) throws biscuit on the floor.

   MOTHER: "What's that? Biscuit on the floor? Where biscuits aren't supposed to be. Isn't it?"

   Child looks at mother and nods.

   MOTHER: "Yes. Now what's all this?" (points to toothbrush and toothpaste on kitchen table). "Who brought that downstairs?"

   Child looks at mother and smiles.

   MOTHER: "Yes, you did. Where does this live?"

   CHILD: "Bath."

2. Sibling of child (24 months) draws on a piece of jigsaw puzzle. Sibling shows mother.

   SIBLING (to mother): Look.

   MOTHER TO SIBLING: "You're not supposed to draw on them. You should know better. You only draw on pieces of paper. You don't draw on puzzles."

   CHILD (to mother): "Why?"

   MOTHER: (to child): "Because they aren't pieces of paper."

   CHILD: "Naughty."

   MOTHER: "Yes that is a naughty thing to do."[3]

Both of these examples show parents instructing children on common family rules. The two rules in question are "Put things where they belong," and "Don't write on things that aren't pieces of paper." In the first example, the child under observation is the transgressor, whereas in the second example the observed child only witnesses and comments upon on a sibling's transgression. What the two cases have in common is that in both a child is familiarized with an unwritten principle of household regulation. Dunn's observations show an enormous amount of such learning during the second year of life.

How do parents go about making their children aware of unwritten rules? The first example reveals a technique that Dunn found to be among the most common and effective among the families that she observed. "Rather than simply stating the rule, the comments (pointing out the rule) were usually in question form, as if the mothers expected and made 'space' for an answer."[4] Through this kind of Socratic "conversation," the child is led first to giving an example of the rule and then to formulating it in a general way.

From the age of sixteen months onwards, parents engage their children in such conversations with increasing frequency. Where appropriate, the parent may also justify the rule in terms of a sibling's feelings. For example, a parent may refer to a rule against taking another person's things and explain it by saying that the child's sibling would be upset if the child used the sibling's toy without asking first. Dunn believes that this too is a highly effective strategy for helping children understand and accept social rules. Clearly it supports the child's own natural empathic leanings. In a follow-up study, Dunn and Penny Munn found that children who acted most socially mature (with more conciliatory behavior, less teasing with peers, and less prohibited behavior) were children whose parents were most likely to communicate with about rules and the feelings of siblings.[5]

The parent is not the only socializing agent in the family. Siblings often take part in reprimanding one another for breaking rules. Sometimes this is done out of genuine dismay at a forbidden act; other times it is simply part of the child's ongoing efforts to tease a sibling. In the second example above, it seems that as soon as the child has learned the rule under discussion, he joins the mother's efforts to enforce it. The entire family is a network in which any member can place pressure on any other member to comply with accepted family regulations.

Not all family communications lead in fact to compliance. Especially when they are young, children tend to ignore messages that they do not want to hear, such as a demand to stop performing a pleasurable but prohibited act. They are, however, well tuned in to verbal and facial emotional expressions, and respond quickly to anger on the part of a parent. By the second year of life children actively monitor their parents' faces and voices for emotional signals.[6] Communications highly charged with affect are likely to draw their attention.

Dunn reports that the children she observed became most acutely aware of a rule when it was conveyed by the parent with intense negative affect. Similarly, observational studies by Robert Emde have shown that before age two, children generally ignore their parents' commands unless the commands are vigorously pressed with a strong emotional overtone.[7] It is not until well after this time, when children themselves have internalized family rules, that there is a reliable tendency to comply voluntarily. And even then, as every parent knows, such compliance is hardly perfect.

Parental emotions like anger and disgust play a role in communicating to children the urgency of following important rules. But this does not mean that greater displays of parental affect lead to ever greater rule following. Continual, strident expressions of anger are likely to bring about just the opposite. As they become commonplace, such expressions lose their ability to arouse attention; and they create an unruly atmosphere that leads to more rather than less disorder in the family. Further, children are likely to imitate parental outbursts in their own behavior, again to the detriment of household harmony and order. Far more effective for capturing the child's attention in a productive manner are "modulated" emotional expressions that follow directly from genuine provocations on the part of the child. Such modulated expressions not only convey a precise message about wrongdoing and its consequences, but they are also within an affective range that the child can tolerate without tuning out.

Even within middle-class Western family life, parents vary widely in how they communicate about rules of conduct and express emotional reactions to breaches. When variations of economic background, ethnicity, and culture are considered, still sharper differences emerge in these and other child-rearing practices. Some of these differences greatly affect the quality and substance of children's morality. They also provide us with clues about which kinds of social environments may be most conducive to children's moral growth.

Some parents are highly punitive, emphasizing the sanctions that follow prohibited behavior. Others lean more towards persuasion of one kind or another. Some parents regularly "set limits" in order to restrict their children's behavioral choices; others permit their children to express their own values and desires freely. Such differences can be extreme or slight. They can combine with one another, and with other child-rearing patterns, to create a particular style of moral discourse in each family. In some families there is an overall consistency in the child-rearing practice; in others, styles are irregular and inconsistent: families also vary in the extent to which they conduct themselves in a stable as opposed to a fluctuating and inconsistent manner.

There is also much variation in the way that parents act from situation to situation. A father who has just lost his job may be more punitive than during times when he feels fewer career pressures. A child who is sick may find her misdeeds greeted more tolerantly than when she was well. Further, the same parents may treat a first-born differently than a second-born child; or a male child differently than a female child; or a shy child differently than an aggressive one.

It is clear from all this that no two children encounter the same pattern of family experience. Since moral rules and values are communicated to young children primarily in the family context, this means that there must be great variation in how children are introduced to these values. There is also great variation in the specific composition of the values that are introduced. Studies with young children and their families have shown that all of these variations can seriously affect the quality and course of children's moral development. But the moral influence of family child-rearing style is not always the same as popular preconceptions might lead us to believe. A good example of this concerns the much-discussed dimension of parental permissiveness.

In the popular culture, much is made of how permissive or restrictive parents are in enforcing behavioral standards. Depending upon which editorial page columnist one reads, all of our society's current shortcomings can be blamed either on the leniency or strictness with which we have raised our children. In fact, each end of the permissiveness/restrictiveness polarity has gone in and out of vogue several times during the past century. In the course of such shifts in fashion, the media—sometimes inaccurately—have taken child care experts such as John D. Watson and Benjamin Spock to represent one or the other pole. These controversies generally assume that the tone of a child's moral character will be set by the relative permissiveness or restrictiveness of a parent.

Scientific research challenges this assumption. Permissiveness and restrictiveness may play a part within a larger context of parental styles, but in themselves they do not have a direct or predictable influence on children's morality. For example, one of the early studies on this topic, conducted by Robert Sears and his colleagues at Stanford, showed that the relative permissiveness of a parent did not have a noticeable effect on a child's tendency to be aggressive.[8] Only when combined with the parent's degree of punitiveness did permissiveness make a difference. Parents who were *both* permissive and punitive tended to have markedly more aggressive children than either parents who were one and not the other or those who were neither. This combination signifies a parental style that is generally lenient, paying little attention to children's breaches except when they directly affect the parent. But when the breach does annoy the parent, the parent reacts with severe punitive measures. It is this inconsistent and self-indulgent form of parenting that Sears and his colleagues, and other researchers,[9] have found linked with children's aggressiveness. In fact, most studies have found that it is always selective *combinations* of parental practices, rather than single dimensions, that influence children's moral values and behavior.[10] The question that we must answer is, Which combinations are beneficial and which ones are deleterious?

Back in the 1940s, Alfred Baldwin conducted a classic study of family life and its consequences for children's development.[11] Baldwin compared families who conducted their affiars "democratically" (frequently communicating about family rules and policy decisions) with families who were more closed, secretive, and arbitrary about decisions. He also looked at the extent to which these parents effectively controlled their children's conduct. He found that children from families with democracy *without* control were often cruel and disobedient, while children in families with control *without* democracy often lacked initiative and an inner sense of responsibility. The combination of democracy *and* control in the family led to an optimal pattern of assertive kindliness on the part of the child.

More recently, Diana Baumrind has reported similar findings, using somewhat different language to describe them.[12] Baumrind's main categorical distinction is between *authoritarian* and *authoritative* patterns of child rearing. Authoritarian child rearing is a combination of high control and low clarity of communication between parent and child. The authoritarian parent also shuns warmth and nurturance while expecting socially mature behavior. Authoritative child rearing, on the other hand is a combination of high control and clear communication. It also favors warmth and nurturance, while still holding firm and consistent maturity expectations. Both patterns contrast, each in its own way, with permissiveness, which combines *low* control with infrequent maturity demands, but also includes clear communication as well as warmth and nurturance.

Like Baldwin, Baumrind found that parents who clearly communicated with their children while at the same time exerting control and demanding maturity (the "authoritative" ones) frequently had children with an active sense of social responsibility. These children were "friendly rather than hostile to peers, facilitative rather than disruptive of others' work, and cooperative rather than resistive of adult-led activity."[13]

Authoritative parents produce socially responsible children for a number of reasons.[14] First, these parents support the child's natural empathic responses by explicitly confronting children about actions that may be harmful to others. Second, they consistently enforce their commands, thus demonstrating their decisive commitment to these commands. Third, they are direct and honest about their commands rather than indirect or manipulative. Fourth, these parents communicate to their children a general norm requiring obedience to authority, along with the sense that good behavior (and the child's identity as a "good" child) requires compliance with legitimate authority. Fifth, their consistent use of parental authority makes them attractive role models for their children.

Further, authoritative parents impose demands that are challenging but not unrealistic.[15] They push their children to improve their behavior, and this may result in some pressure and some clash of will; but because authoritative parents are also communicative and responsive, they continually tailor their demands to the child's capabilities. This makes their demands moderately, but not overly, tension-producing for the child, an ideal spur for development.[16]

In contrast, both authoritarian and permissive parents shield their children from challenging stress. The former do so by limiting their children's opportunities for exploration, the latter by not confronting their children with the adverse effects of their own acts. As a consequence, children from these two very different family backgrounds have similar difficulties in developing self-reliance, assertiveness, an autonomous sense of social responsibility, and a tolerance for life's ups and downs. Baumrind found a similar pattern of low self-control and lack of initiative among children from both authoritarian and permissive families. This pattern of similarity is somewhat surprising, since these two parenting styles seem so radically opposed to one another. But in fact both sets of parents make essentially the same two mistakes: First, they fail to confront children regularly and consistently about moral transgressions, and second, they overintrude into the child's own experience.

Authoritarian and permissive parents make these mistakes quite differently. Authoritarian parents fail to confront children in a regular and consistent manner because authoritarian directives stem from the parents' own moods and temper. The coercive harshness of these parents reflects their own egocentric needs rather than objective assessments of the child's behavior. Such harshness leads to arbitrary intrusions into the child's life.

Permissive parents, in contrast, are philosophically or temperamentally disinclined towards discipline. As a result, they avoid any confrontations over the child's transgressions. Yet they, too, intrude in their own way. The intrusion of permissive parents takes the form of a sentimental overprotectiveness rather than coercion and punishment. The child is sheltered from experiencing unpleasantness of any type, even when this unpleasantness is simply a realistic consequence of the child's bad behavior. In many cases, permissive parents also find ways of preventing teachers and other authority figures from forcing the child to face such consequences. These parents intrude into their children's school and peer relationships whenever they fear that their children may need protection from a possibly harsh experience. Although this looks like a gentler and more caring form of intrusiveness than the authoritarian mode, the adverse effects on children's self-control and initiative are the same.

Baumrind's work shows how the "authoritative" pattern of firm parental control mixed with responsiveness, clear communication, and maturity demands can foster social responsibility (as well as competence) in children. Authoritative parenting may not be the only means of achieving this end.[17] In fact, Baumrind's own data reveal a small subset of families in which the same ends were achieved through an entirely "harmonious" set of relations between parent and child.[18] In these families, the parent rarely needs to assert control, because the children anticipate the parent's directives and obey without command or discipline. Like children of authoritative parents, these children from "harmonious" families turned out competent and socially responsible.

Such family patterns may be far more common in Eastern cultures such as Japan than in our own society; indeed, a sizable proportion of the few "harmonious" families in Baumrind's own data base were Japanese-Americans. This suggests that parenting is itself very much influenced by cultural values and practices—a point that we shall return to shortly. It also suggests that there is more than one viable way to support children's moral growth. Baumrind's own conclusion is that authoritative child rearing is *sufficient but not necessary* for encouraging optimal development.[19] It works, but so do family patterns in which children from the start actively assume responsibility for anticipating parental directives and maintaining family order.

As in any communication, the medium is a large part of the message when it comes to influencing children's values. A parent's manner of expressing and enforcing standards of behavior tells the child a great deal about the parent's own values. A parent's communication style also sets an example for the child's expressive behavior in other social relationships. Accompanying all of the family and child-rearing patterns outlined above, there are several distinct means by which parents attempt to communicate moral values to their young. Some procedures have proven more effective than others for the establishment of long-lasting behavioral standards in children.

Martin Hoffman has identified *power assertion, love withdrawal,* and *induction* as three basic techniques parents can use to transmit values to their children.[20] Power assertion means employing force or punishment as the main means of ensuring the child's compliance with parental standards. In power assertion, the parent's command is justified through the parent's power to enforce rather than through any intrinsic value that the command might have: it is a familial form of might makes right. Love withdrawal means expressing disapproval or disappointment when a child deviates from the standards. This can be accomplished through direct statements—"I don't like you when you act like that"—or through a cold glance or grimace. Induction means ensuring the child's compliance through some form of control, but at the same time drawing the child's attention to the reasons behind the standard. For young children, this often entails giving information about how bad behavior adversely affects others. For example, one common induction used by many parents is to stop a child from pushing his sibling while telling him, "If you keep pushing her like that, she may fall down and cry."

Research has shown that power assertion is a good way of stopping children from doing something dangerous to themselves or others *in the short term*. It may be necessary if a child is about to run into the street or hit her brother on the head with a hammer, but is ineffective for creating permanent change in a child's conduct and values. Once the asserter of power is no longer present, the child tends to revert to the old standards. Without the continued presence of constraint, there is little continued compliance.

In fact, power assertion that is too strenuous may actually *decrease* the child's tendency to follow parental standards. In one clever experiment, one group of children was forbidden to play with a toy in a mild way, while a second group was forbidden the toy under threat of severe punishment.[21] On a later occasion, the children returned to the laboratory and were observed as they approached the forbidden toy. Children from the severe-threat group frequently played with the toy when they thought no one was looking, whereas children from the mild constraint group often said that the toy was boring and not worth playing with. If anything, therefore, severe threats are counterproductive to lasting social influence.

Love withdrawal produces behavioral changes that are somewhat longer lasting. Experimental findings have shown that it can be used successfully in teaching children to inhibit their hostile urges towards others.[22] Children whose parents consistently rely on love withdrawal as a disciplinary technique often are self-controlled and respectful of the rights and property of others. But even though it can have an enduring positive effect on children's behavior, love withdrawal does not lead children to develop fully autonomous moral beliefs that they consider their own. Instead, it creates a need for children to conform to parental standards for the sake of their parent's approval. Such a need indeed may continue to assert itself even in the parent's absence, thus motivating the child to maintain her good behavior over time. But this still does not have the staying power of the child's own deep-seated belief in the behavioral standard itself.

Only induction has been found to foster such internalized beliefs. Children exposed to frequent inductions during disciplinary encounters tend to adopt their parents standards as their own. The standards become "functionally autonomous." That is, the standards operate on their own far into the future, despite the parent's absence—and even despite a parent's subsequent disavowal of the standard. For example, a child in whom a parent had successfully induced the standard of honesty could become quite offended later in life if the same parent claimed that cheating on taxes was fine. The standard now exists on its own, wholeheartedly adopted by the child, independent of further parental input.

In general, the optimal conditions for the successful induction of moral beliefs are (1) control of the child's behavior through the minimal external force necessary for achieving such control, combined with (2) provision of information to the child about the rationale for the standard through persuasion, argument, and reasoning.

Control is needed because mere instruction without ensuring behavioral compliance does not "stick." Children quickly forget the message unless they are made to act accordingly. With control, the theory goes, the child performs the proper behavior out of necessity and then gradually begins to believe in the standard represented by this behavior. It is the parent's firm control combined with input about the rationale behind the standard that produces this "internalized" belief. But the parent's control cannot be too forceful: if so, it will remain salient in the child's mind, and force will be all the child remembers from the disciplinary encounter. The goal is to have the child act properly and then to come away from the event remembering why it was important to do so. This is only possible if the informational message is more memorable for the child than the sanctions used to enforce it. The key here is presenting a moral rationale along with a mild form of coercion, so that the child mainly retains the rationale.

The "forbidden toy" experiment provides us with a compelling demonstration of this principle. Mark Lepper and his colleagues have shown that this principle works in the case of positive as well as negative incentives.[23] In other words, inducing children towards behavioral standards through rewards is best done with minimal reward, just as inducing them through enforced control is best done with minimal force. Lepper asked three groups of children to play with Magic Markers, an activity that they normally enjoy on their own. The first two groups were given attractive rewards (a "Good Player" certificate) after they had finished. The third group was given nothing. Weeks later all the children were brought back to the laboratory and given a chance to play with the Magic Markers again if they wanted to. Only the third group leaped at this opportunity. Lepper concluded that he had diminished the autonomous, intrinsic motivation of children in the first two groups by offering them "an unnecessarily salient extrinsic incentive."[24]

These experimental findings may help us better understand the effects of the different child-rearing patterns described by Diana Baumrind. Authoritarian parents rely on coercive disciplinary techniques that are too strenuous and therefore too salient. These parents may get their children to comply in the short run, but over the long haul there is nothing to sustain the desired standard. Permissive parents, on the other hand, fail to provide their children with even the minimum coercions or rewards necessary to change the child's behavior in the first place. Thus, in the end, both sets of parents often see their children engaging in unruly behavior. Authoritative parents combine mild enforcement techniques with clear reasoning and argument. This establishes ideal conditions for children to internalize socially appropriate standards. Hence Baumrind's claim that children whose parents raise them in an authoritative manner are likely to perform socially responsible acts on their own initiative throughout life.

It is important, however, for parents not to allow mild enforcement to become deceitful manipulation by covering up its source or existence—for example, by telling a child that he stopped hitting his sister because he loves her when the real reason was that his father grabbed him and sent him to his room. In other words, parents must represent honestly the extent to which the child is indeed being coerced even if this is an aspect of the encounter that the parent would just as soon have the child forget. Deceiving children into behaving correctly by misrepresenting the situation is objectionable for several reasons, both practical and moral. First, deception as an influence strategy is impractical in the long run, because sooner or later children realize that they are being manipulated. Children, in fact, are keenly aware of "tricks" from an early age.[25] If parents or other adults consistently relied on getting children to misperceive events as part of their moral instruction, children would quickly develop a mistrust for the entire enterprise (as well as for the adults involved). Fortunately, real-life parenting in this case does not often emulate experimenters' manipulative designs.

Further, social influence is generally not accomplished through calculated strategies foisted upon unsuspecting recipients. Rather, it normally comes about through a series of negotiations, cooperative or otherwise, between persons who may or may not be aware that they are influencing one another—and who, as a rule, give little thought to how influence is strategically accomplished.

As a rule, too, moral ends do not derive from immoral means. I do not write this to sermonize, but rather to indicate that what we have here is yet another example of this powerful axiom. Deception cannot work as a means of moral influence because children are not dumb creatures who remain permanently unaware of deceptive practices. Even if a deceptive practice is successful at gaining a child's behavioral compliance, it spins off unwanted messages and other dangerous byproducts. One such message is that dishonesty is condoned by the adults whom one most respects. Diana Baumrind sums up the danger here:

> Manipulative parents are likely to produce manipulative
> children. Parents' subtle manipulation of children's motivation
> provides a model for dishonest behavior, which is likely to be
> detected by children in the home setting.[26]

Because children act as intelligent participants in their social relationships, attempts to influence them must respect their awareness and their many capabilities. This does not mean that children must be given free rein. We have seen that firm parental control can provide important guidance for the child's moral development. But such control is effective only when it is communicated to children openly and directly. It is most effective when coupled with parental reasoning that supports rather than disregards the child's own moral inclinations.

Children not only participate actively in their social relationships; they also develop their own beliefs about these relationships. Such beliefs derive very much from children's own cognitive perspectives: they are not simply a blind reflection of what others would have children believe. This is as much true for children's beliefs about adult-child relations as for their beliefs about any other social relations.

There is a natural developmental progression in the way that children think about adult authority. Children at all ages believe that obeying authority is important. But as they grow older, children change their reasons for obeying, as well as their choices about whom to obey, and under what conditions. These attitudinal changes engender increasingly open and mature (though also increasingly confrontational) adult-child exchanges as children move into adolescence.

Much as in studies of children's early sharing conceptions, children's ideas about authority have been explored by using hypothetical stories and extended questions.[27] One story used for children between the ages of four and twelve is the following:

> This is Peter (Michelle for girl subjects) and here is his mother, Mrs. Johnson (pictures of story characters are shown). Mrs. Johnson wants Peter to clean up his own room every day, and she tells him that he can't go out and play until he cleans his room up and straightens out his toys. But one day Peter's friend Michael comes over and tells Peter that all the kids are leaving right away for a picnic. Peter wants to go, but his room is a big mess. He tells his mother that he doesn't have time to straighten his room right now, but he'll do it later. She says no, he'll have to stay and miss the picnic.[28]

This story, and others like it, are followed by questions that probe children's ideas about the *legitimacy* of authority (the bases for the authority figure's right to command) and about the *rationale for obedience* (why it is important to do as the authority figure says). Typical questions along these lines are: "What is it about parents that gives them the right to tell kids what to do?" "Why would it be wrong for Peter to ignore his mother and go out anyway?" As the following quotes illustrate, children's answers to such questions change dramatically in the years between infancy and adolescence.

Until age five or so, children believe that they obey because they want to. There is only a shaky understanding that some commands conflict with one's desires and still must be followed. The two children quoted directly below are both four-year-olds:

> Is it all right for Peter's mother to say that? *No.* Why not? *Because he can't go out to play.* But he didn't clean his room like she asked him to. Does that make it all right for her to say

that? *No.* Why not? *She wouldn't say something like that.* She wouldn't? Why not? *Her mother only tells him to do good things.*

What do you think Peter should do? *Go to the picnic.* Why should he do that? *Because he wants to and all his friends are going.* But what if his mother says, "No, Peter, you can't go until you clean up your room first?" *He would do what his mom says.* What if Peter really wants to go on the picnic and he doesn't want to clean up his room at all because if he does he'll miss the picnic? *His mommy will let him go out with his friends.* But what if she won't let him? *He will stay home and play with his sister and clean up all his toys in his toy box.* Why will he do that? *Because he wants to.*[29]

By the end of the preschool years, children come more to terms with the realities of parent-child conflict and impending punishment. Parental authority is legitimized by size, strength, and other indications of power. The unpleasant consequences of disobedience provide a forceful rationale for obeying. A fairly typical quote from a five-year-old is the following:

What should Peter do? *Clean up his room.* Why should he do that? *Because his mother told him to.* Why does he have to do what his mother tells him to? *Because she's the mother.* What difference does that make? *'Cause she's the boss of the house like his father.* What makes them the boss of the house? *Mothers and fathers are bigger and they can spank.*[30]

Children soon learn that parents have more to recommend them than brute strength and power. By middle childhood there is an awareness of other parental virtues that legitimize their authority. Most prominent among these are their superior intelligence and know-how. Obedience is considered a sign of respect for the parent's abilities. It also has a certain reciprocal value: one obeys not only as a necessary gesture of respect, but also as a kind of payback for the parents' protection and nurturance. Because the parent knows a lot, the parent is in a good position to help you, and that fact alone dictates obedience. The following quotes are from three children ages seven and eight:

Why is it important to do what your mother says? *Because if it's something that you can't do she might help you.* Is that why you do what she tells you to? *Yes, she's the one that can help you the most.* Why is she the one that can help you like that? *Well, she's older and can do a lot of things you can't do.*

What should Peter do? *He should miss the picnic.* How come? *Because if his mother told him to do something he should do it.* Why? *Because if you were sick and asked her for a glass of water she would do it for you.*

What if Peter sneaks out of the house and goes on the picnic anyway? *He shouldn't do that.* Why not? *'Cause his mother told him to stay in and clean his room.* Well, why should he do what his mother says? *Because she's the one taking care of him.* What difference does that make? *Well, after all she's done for him it just doesn't seem fair that he wouldn't do what she says.*[31]

Towards the end of childhood, there is a growing sense that obeying parental authority is in one's best interests because parents care about their children and have more experience than they do. But at the same time there is also a growing sense of equality in the relationship. When the parent is wrong, the child has a right to disagree. At the threshold of adolescence, many children express the belief that obedience is a matter of choice, a voluntary deferral to someone with leadership qualities who cares about one's welfare. There is a situational quality to this choice: should a child know more than the parent about a certain matter, the parent should listen to the child on this topic. The following remarks are from a nine-year-old, but are more typical of children some years older:

Why does Peter have to listen to his mother? *Because she knows what's best for him.* Is that why she's telling him to clean his room? *Well, she knows it's best for him to learn to do stuff like that.* How does she know that? *'Cause she's a mother and she's learned all about how to raise kids.* What if it were something she didn't know about? Like, suppose the whole family went on a camping trip and nobody knew about camping, nobody had gone camping before except Peter. *Then they should all listen to Peter and he should tell them what to do.* They should all listen to what Peter says? *If he knows the most about camping.* Why should they? *He knows what to do, he should lead the way, and his mother and father better listen.*[32]

Towards the end of childhood, therefore, authority begins to be seen as a consensual relation that serves the interests of all who participate in it. This is a far more constructive way of viewing authority than the respect-for-power perspective of younger children. For one thing, it encourages a voluntary spirit of obedience. For another thing, it further opens the channels of communication between parent and child. When children engage in genuine two-way dialogues with parents about choices and values, the parents' opinions are usually heard and taken seriously. When parents' opinions are unilaterally dictated and couched in a context of coercion, they are often lost in the surrounding noise.

Perhaps most importantly, the developing child's new views on authority relations pave the way for a social perspective that will be necessary for adaptation to civilized living. All societies need to delegate authority and need to have such delegations followed and respected. The older child begins to see the social rationale for systems of leadership and followership. Further, the older child understands that authority is legitimate only when it serves the interests of subordinate as well as leader; and that this means that authority figures must have claims to special qualities like experience or talent that enable them to lead effectively. By this logic, children can imagine themselves in leadership positions someday, a sure sign of impending preparation for full citizenship in society.

The important changes that I have described in children's views on authority are natural and widespread, but particular family settings can foster them to a greater or lesser extent. As research has shown, families with clear communication between parent and child–as in Baumrind's "authoritative" pattern of child rearing—are far more conducive to the development of mature beliefs about authority than are families in which parents act in a harshly coercive or laxly permissive manner. In this sense, there is a two-way interplay between children's beliefs and the family atmosphere. In highly communicative families, children readily develop mature ideas about authority; and as children develop more mature authority beliefs, the family atmosphere becomes more democratic and communicative.[33]

In family life around the world, there are wide variations in how parents communicate moral values to their children, as well as in the nature of the values that they choose to express. The most striking contrast is that our own culture promotes the values of independence, liberty, and assertiveness, whereas many others promote the values of interdependence, community, and tradition. Whereas many urban Western societies tend to be similar to our own in this regard, many agrarian sections of Africa, India, and

Asia tend to be among the latter (see, for example, the Chapter 6 discussion of children's morality in parts of India).

Beatrice and John Whiting and their colleagues have compared family life in cultural settings as diverse as Okinawa, Mexico, the Philippines, India, Kenya, and New England.[34] They report that children in the United States are weaned earlier and isolated more from the community at large than in any other culture they have studied. Throughout development, they are encouraged to excel over others rather than to blend in with the needs and traditions of the community. All of this has the effect of encouraging autonomy and self-assertiveness in Western children, at the expense of a shared sense of solidarity with others.

The Whitings also found that children in the rural societies they studied—the Philippine, Kenyan, and Mexican children—behave more altruistically than do children from urban societies—the U.S., Okinawan, and Indian children in the Whitings' sample. In rural families, mothers often work in the fields during the day. The children therefore must take on serious household chores and other family responsibilities. They baby-sit with younger siblings and help with the wash and cooking. They even assist with care of the sick and elderly. Such frequent helping activity can accustom children to prosocial behavior as a habitual mode of conduct.

Urban children, particularly in technological societies like the United States, assume relatively little responsibility in the family. One effect of this may be the urban child's propensity towards competitiveness rather than cooperation as a social standard. The anthropologist Millard Madsen conducted several studies contrasting urban and rural children around the world on this dimension, consistently finding the urban children to be more competitive and conflictual and the rural children to be more cooperative and generous in their social interactions.[35]

An important early difference between Western and non-Western children is that the former are far more prone to attention-seeking ("Look at me, Mommy!") than the latter. Studies in Africa by Robert LeVine suggest ways in which parental styles may combine with cultural values to produce such contrasts.[36] LeVine reports that African parents rarely praise their children for good behavior. Rather, they communicate the message that such behavior is to be expected. This means that behavior that conforms to parental standards is largely ignored, whereas deviations from the standards are punished: "Children in those societies observe and imitate, getting corrective feedback when necessary and no feed-back when they perform correctly." This, of course, stands in sharp contrast to middle-class American parental communication, which rewards children's good behavior with compliments. LeVine believes that such parental praise only increases the child's tend-ency to demonstrate the behavior in front of the parent and de-creases the child's compliance with parental requests and com-mands. In addition, parental praise encourages attention-seeking as a generalized mode of activity.

Attention-seeking is an early form of the assertiveness that many parents in our culture intentionally inculcate in their young. Most people in our achievement-oriented society consider assertiveness to be a virtue. It is related to self-confidence, and contributes to personal competence and success. But assertiveness sometimes works agaisnt virtues like humility, deference, and self-sacrifice that are more highly valued in cultures that stress the interdepen-dence of persons. Parents in such cultures do not seek to nurture early manifestations of assertiveness such as attention-seeking.

In child-rearing practices, we can see cultures maintaining them-selves by transmitting their values to new generations. The trans-mission of values is not done directly, through lectures or lessons about right and wrong. Rather, it is accomplished through the sub-tle encouragement or discouragement of behaviors such as atten-tion-seeking. Parents around the world must have an intuitive ability to recognize implications for the culture's heritage in such childhood behaviors.

No society, of course, is a homogeneous whole when it comes to values. Individuals within any society disagree about what is right and wrong, just as they disagree about the best way to raise moral children. Any picture of cultural contrasts is painted with a broad brush, covering over many within-culture inconsistencies. Further, societies change, sometimes acquiring radically new val-ues in the space of one or two generations. This century has wit-nessed many traditional societies taking on Western values. In some cases, reactions within these societies have led to a rejection of the changes and a reassertion of the old values. In other cases, the tension between the two continues and acts as a socially divi-sive force.

A recent study by psychologists in mainland China offers us a vivid account of how a society in transition struggles to foster moral values in its children.[37] Professors Jiao, Ji, and Jing were interested in the developmental effects of China's one-child family policy. This policy, implemented by a centralized State Family Planning Commission, has succeeded in dramatically reducing the size of many Chinese families. According to recent surveys, almost three-fourths of married couples in China's major cities and provinces now have only one child. Political leaders in China believe that this shift will have salutary economic consequences. Professors Jiao, Ji, and Jing were curious about the consequences for Chinese children.

The researchers studied almost a thousand kindergarten and elementary school children from rural and urban backgrounds. Children with siblings were compared with only children on a range of social and cognitive dimensions. The researchers went into the children's schools and asked the children's peers to rate how cooperative, friendly, or selfish the children were. In both rural and urban settings, only children were found to be more self-centered than children with siblings. They acted more according to their own interests and tended to share and cooperate less with others. Children with siblings were better liked by their peers and more able to cope with constraints and frustrations.

The researchers conclude that, at least in China, a family environment with siblings is an important part of a child's moral upbringing. "Communal home life," they write, "requires cooperation and collective participation."[38] Children are forced to share their parents' attention with their brothers or sisters and must learn to respond productively to peer pressure. Only children are at a disadvantage here. The researchers cite one observation of "an only child in a kindergarten who did not know how to put his clothes on after the noon nap; he just sat on the bed waiting for the nurse to dress him. If no one came to attend to him, he would just sit there, watching the others get dressed."[39]

Such problems exist in many places around the world. The Whitings have found that only children are less inclined to share and help than are children with younger siblings. But this seems to be the case mainly in the rural and traditional cultures where children in general tend to be more cooperative and altruistic. It does not seem that only children in contemporary America or other urban Western cultures are markedly more egocentric than their peers from large families. It may be that parents in rural societies do not try as hard as their urban counterparts to compensate for the only child's lack of peer influences.

This problem may be particularly aggravated in a society like China, where the shift to small families has been sudden and mandated. It may be that there has not been enough time for the culture to develop ways of orienting children to prosocial values in the absence of the large family experience.

One can imagine why this research report has created concern among Chinese policy makers. The nation's socialist ethic could not long endure an entire generation of self-centered individualists. If Chinese children are indeed being unintentionally trained to eschew communal values, they will inevitably clash with their culture's primary values at some point in their development. Indeed, there are already reports that contemporary Chinese youth, to the distress of many of their elders, are increasingly attracted to materialism, individualistic achievement, and other Western values. Changing family structure, and the altered early experience that it brings, could be one reason behind this new attraction.

Every society undergoes some generational flux in values: this is how cultures change over time. Parents, it seems, only partially succeed in replicating their own values in the young. This is because even the most effective parents are not perfect inducers of values; and there are many parental practices and family conditions that are ineffective—or even counterproductive. Carolyn Pope Edwards, for example, has described a Kenyan tribe where parents strenuously discourage aggression in their children by beating offenders.[40] Not surprisingly, children from this tribe frequently resort to hitting when confronted with a problem, despite the behavioral standard advocated by their parents.

There is also generational flux because parents are not the only influences on children's moral development. Children often sort out matters of right and wrong among themselves in the context of the social realities within which they find themselves. In so doing, they often come to their own conclusions, regardless of what their parents might say. There is much in the way of moral experience that children encounter outside the home, as we shall see in the next chapter.

5

·

Interacting as Equals
Cooperative Play
in the Peer Group

At its best, friendship can create an ideal moral condition. In true friendship, the welfare of one party is seen as synonymous with the welfare of the other. Joys and sorrows are shared, and loyalty is assumed. Conflicts of interest are resolved with a sympathetic understanding of the other's perspective. In true friendship, there is a spontaneous respect for the other's rights and a responsive concern for the other's well-being. Accordingly, fairness between friends does not need to be mandated, but rather arises readily from the relationship. This is no doubt what Aristotle meant by the following bit of widsom: "When people are friends, they have no need of justice, but when they are just, they need friendship in addition."

Childhood is a time of burgeoning friendships. The formation of friendships comes naturally to children: in fact, this is one of a child's keenest interests as early as toddlerhood.[1] During the years immediately following infancy, children spend increasing amounts of time with peers. In the process, they begin to establish and maintain close peer relationships. The earliest forms of these relationships are by no means models of true friendship, but with age children acquire the knowledge and personal experience necessary for conducting stable relations with close and intimate friends.

Even the earliest friendships have unwritten standards of conduct as well as expected responsibilities. Children learn about these as they experience the ups and downs of their friendships—both the ones that work and the ones that break down. As a consequence, some central elements of morality are first discovered through play with friends. It may well be, in fact, that friendship

73

is the primary context in which children acquire certain key behavioral norms and moral standards.

Bronwyn Davies, an Australian researcher, observed patterns of
children's play in her native country and questioned the children
about the meaning of their social interactions.[2] In her observations,
Davies was struck by the strength and coherence of children's own
culture, which includes clear norms and prescriptions for peer relationships. These norms and prescriptions sometimes parallel,
sometimes differ from, and sometimes oppose the standards represented in adult societal interchange. Where children perceive a
difference, their loyalty often tends to be directed toward the peer
standards. As a consequence, their behavior is often guided more
by the expectations of their friends than by standards that they
have learned from adults.

Recall the Chapter 1 example of Hartshorne and May's studies
on childhood character. In these experiments, childhood honor
(helping a peer) was unintentionally set against an adult standard
(not cheating on a seemingly arbitrary task). As in many real-life
incidents, childhood honor between peers prevailed—to the apparent mystification of the adult experimenters.

Many of the childhood norms and standards that I discuss below
continue to be essential in adulthood as well. This, in fact, is one
reason why childhood peer relations are so important in preparing
children for adult social life. But children carry out these norms
and standards in their own way, which often bears little resemblance to the ways of adults. Adult versions of moral norms and
standards do not always translate well to childhood culture. As a
consequence, adults often find their lectures about fairness or honesty falling on deaf ears. Only when children discover these norms
and standards in their own social play do they begin to realize
their value.

The primary norm of childhood culture is reciprocity. In itself,
this does not distinguish childhood from adulthood, for reciprocity is the fundamental fact of all human interchange. Moreover,
this fundamental fact is as old as civilization itself. Robert Cairns,
emphasizing reciprocity's elemental role in social and moral exchange, has quoted the following Confucian analect:

Tse-Kung put to him the question, "Is there one word upon
which the whole life may proceed?" The Master replied, "Is

not reciprocity such a word?—What you do not yourself desire, do not put before others."[3]

An ancient Western version of this analect is the biblical Golden Rule ("Do unto others as you would have them do unto you"). Despite differences in theological heritage, the core message in both is the same: moral living revolves around the assumption that social actions are reciprocal. This assumption has implications for one's conduct towards others as well as for one's expectations concerning others' conduct towards oneself. One therefore takes responsibility for the former and asserts rights with regard to the latter; and these responsibilities and rights exist in a reciprocal relation to one another.

Reciprocity in social relationships can be defined most simply as a multifaceted principle of give and take. It is fundamental for social relationships because it is needed to establish, maintain, and repair them. Of all social norms, reciprocity is the only one that is absolutely necessary for the very existence of relationships.

Reciprocity establishes relationships by making communication possible. There could be no "conversation" of any kind—neither verbal nor nonverbal—without some two-way exchange of gestures, meaningful responses, and other mutual expressions of recognition that meaning has been exchanged. We know that these kinds of reciprocal exchanges occur very early in life, in the infant's interactions with caregivers shortly after birth.[4] They recur in more and more elaborate form with each new relationship that the child establishes.

Once relationships are established, reciprocity maintains them by ensuring that exchanges eventually serve the interests of both parties. This provides a balance of interest in the relationship that prevents it from breaking down. When, however, acts of injury or insult do temporarily destroy the relationship, reciprocity can repair it through compensatory acts. Such acts might include material reparations, apologies, expressions of forgiveness, or the giving and taking of retribution. Some forms of reciprocity are typical of certain childhood relations and some are not. Of particular significance to moral development, children's peer relations foster a type of "direct" reciprocity that is relatively rare in most adult-child relationships.

In her observations of children's social play, Davies identified two examples of reciprocity that are common in children's friend-

ships.[5] The first is a reciprocation of judgment: "I am a mirror
to you which provides you with my perception of your behavior
towards me."[6] The second is a reciprocation of action: "I should
behave to you as you behave to me. I should reciprocate any
wrongdoing which you do towards me, and, less importantly, I
should reciprocate correct behavior as well."[7]

Both kinds of reciprocity are examples of *direct reciprocity*,[8] in
which each party is free to direct actions and reactions without
constraint by the other party. There is a "symmetry of initiative"
in direct reciprocity.[9] The contrast is *reciprocity by complement*, where
one party's actions and reactions follow the directives of the other
party. Child-child relations generally are characterized by direct
reciprocity, whereas adult-child relations (at least until adolescence) are characterized by reciprocity by complement.[10]

The reason that child-child relations are conducted through direct reciprocity is that children usually perceive each other as
equals in status and power. This is why parties in a childhood
friendship feel that they can give and receive directives to one
another without hesitation. As a rule, close childhood friendships
are based on an assumption of equality, and the desire to have such
friendships strongly motivates children to adopt equality as a norm
in their social transactions. When discussing their relations with
friends, children frequently express the standard of equality as a
defining element of the relationship.[11] This tendency increases as
children grow older. Moreover, children come to distinguish between friends and nonfriends on the basis of this defining element.
Reviewing a series of experimental studies, Thomas Berndt concludes that childhood friends show a greater concern for equality
than nonfriends—although Berndt adds the caveat that even in
friendship this concern for equality can be overcome by a spirit
of competition if the situation dictates it.[12]

Beyond reciprocity, children's peer relations promote two other
standards of interpersonal interaction: mutuality and intimacy.
Mutuality means a high level of joint participation in discourse or
other collaborative activities. Intimacy means a close affectionate
bond leading to the shared disclosure of secrets and other confidences. Research has found that children talk more with their
friends than with others, and that friendship talk is "high quality"
talk.[13] It is responsive, rich in fantasy, and revealing of the self's
innermost thoughts and feelings. It is also considerate, even in its
argumentative forms. Where childhood friends disagree, they can

expend great effort explaining and justifying their own positions to one another. This consideration creates the sense of trust that makes the intimate sharing of secrets possible.

Mutuality and intimacy are interpersonal rather than moral standards. They do not, in and of themselves, promote moral concerns like justice, honesty, or kindness. It is possible, for example, to be manipulative and deceitful while at the same time engaging in joint collaborative dialogues with intimate overtones. Still, mutuality and intimacy, because of their interpersonal value, contribute indirectly but importantly to children's moral awareness and learning. They do so in part by creating an intensely emotional tone in children's friendships. Berndt, for example, reports that during childhood, "conversations between friends have more affective impact than conversations with other peers: the highs are higher and the lows are lower."[14] The affective impact, engendered by the marked closeness of the relationship, causes children to pay careful attention to friendship's norms, standards, and rules of procedure. Such careful attention in turn leads children to remember and master the moral standards learned during friendship encounters, setting the stage for the child's later use of these standards all throughout life.

For this reason, children's friendships act as forums for learning moral standards. They are highly effective in large part because children engage so eagerly in them and because the emotional stakes are so high. Children care about their friendships and take seriously the norms and standards expected in the relationship. The moral significance of early friendships is that they provide children with a charged motivational context for discovering and practicing fundamental moral standards. The precise standards that a child learns in friendship may or may not bear close face resemblance to adult moral prescriptions. Nevertheless, these childhood standards often stand as early versions of important moral principles that later will assume a different form. As such, these childhood standards provide necessary precursors—the initial building blocks—of moral maturity.

One of the most important moral standards fostered by children's peer relations is truth. Children confront one another constantly about matters of honesty, communicating an expectation that friends will be open and frank with one another. This provides children with strong incentives to respect and practice honesty in their everyday transactions. Davies observed in childhood culture a common standard of truth that she calls *discoverable facticity*.[15] This standard reflects a belief in a single truth that, when uncovered, will reveal "what happened" in any event. Discovering and honoring such a truth becomes paramount to repairing a friendship that has been disrupted by a grievance. If the events of a conflict can be accurately reconstructed and accepted, clear solutions (like apologizing) can be quickly found. For this reason, children constantly discuss what "really" happened. Lying about events to one's friends is severely discouraged, to the point where this becomes an offense that in itself can impair the relationship.

As noted, such norms and standards as reciprocity, truth, and equality are, in one form or another, as important to adult relationships as to children's. Adults continue (1) to evaluate other people's behavior and to expect such evaluations from others, (2) to respond appropriately to grievances or favors, and to expect such responses from others, (3) to encourage veracity and to discourage dishonesty in their own and others' accounts, and (4) to strive for a sense of equality between themselves and their compatriots. In many ways, these norms and standards are the pillars of civilized life.

But some features of children's friendships are quite different from the features that will characterize their later relationships. The relational norms that belong distinctly to childhood give early friendships a special flavor, sometimes distasteful to us as adults. One distinctly childhood norm is the flexible vacillation of treatment allowed between parties in a friendship; another is the criterion of simple contiguous association for selecting friends.

In children's culture, unacceptable behavior towards a friend (such as hitting) can quickly become appropriate if the friend starts acting badly.[16] This means that children can be kind to their friends one moment and then surprisingly cruel the next moment if their interest in the present situation justifies it. All the while they assume that their friendships will remain intact and that the damage done by the cruelty will be quickly repaired and forgotten. This is quite different from adult relationships, where harsh words or actions between friends can linger and impair the relationship indefinitely. The contrast here between child and adult relationships is one of both belief and fact: not only do children assume that most breaches in their peer relations can be quickly and easily repaired, but in fact this is the case.[17]

Davies observed an example of how children's friendships can combine the common standard of reciprocity with a childhood acceptance of unfriendly behavior within relationships.[18] In Australia there is a game of insults called "sucked in." We do not have "sucked in" in America, but here and everywhere else that there are children parallel versions arise spontaneously. For example, I recently observed American children playing similar verbal games under the delicate phrasing of "chewed up, swallowed down, and spit out by the cat."

The general point of this type of childhood game is to entice a friend to say something stupid and then to make the stupidity public with the cry of "sucked in!" An illustration of this would be the type of dialogue illustrated below.

CHILD 1: I like this kind of bike. Jamie just got one on her birthday.

CHILD 2: Not me. I like the kind made in Italy.

CHILD 1: How come?

CHILD 2: They can ride them faster, like in the races you see.

CHILD 1: Where is Italy anyway?

CHILD 2: You know, it's, um, over in the other side of the world.

CHILD 1: Oh yeah, you mean it's the one near Argentina.

CHILD 2: Yeah, I think so.

CHILD 1: Where they have the pyramids and stuff.

CHILD 2: Um, yeah, yeah.

CHILD 1: Sucked in!

There is some cruelty to this, though not an entirely pointless cruelty. The game's justification usually is that the insulted party had been acting pretentious, prideful, or arrogantly misinformed in some way. Of course the fundamental justification simply can be the reciprocal one of paying back a friend for just having done it to you.

The other norm of childhood friendship that distinguishes early relationships from later ones is the basing of friendships less upon affective preferences (what kind of person you like) than on the simple existence of opportunities to play together. Young children say that they like those with whom they play rather than the other way around. Adolescents and adults, in contrast, choose their friends (as opposed to mere "acquaintances") according to such criteria as similarity and respect; and these choices reflect beliefs about the kinds of people with whom it is most appropriate to share one's affection, confidences, and mutual interests (as opposed to simply one's time or activity).

Through the childhood years, there is a continual development in children's beliefs about the nature of friendship. In the course of this development, children gradually abandon their early assumptions that friendship should be formed through simple contiguous association and conducted as a series of vacillating acts. At the same time, they maintain and expand upon their beliefs in reciprocity, truth, mutuality, and intimacy. Development during the childhood years, therefore, is a matter of abandoning certain norms that apply best to early play associations and enhancing the norms and standards that will be central to the child's mature relationships in later years. The following quotes from interviews with children ages between the ages of five and eleven illustrate these developmental trends.

1 (five years old). Do you have lots of friends? *Chris, Amy, Paula, Bart, and Kevin.* How did you get so many friends? *I got them when I moved into this class.* Are all of your friends in this class? *Yes.* Who's your best friend in your class? *Amy.* Why is Amy your best friend? *I like her. I knew her in . . . [preschool] and I knew her before I came to school.* How did you meet Amy? *We sat on the bus, we played together. . . .* Would you let Amy ride your bike? *Yes, if she came over to my house.* Why would Amy come over to your house? *Because I want her to.* If you had only one bike, would you let Amy ride? *Yeah, I'd take a turn, then she'd take a turn. We'd share it.* Would you share with everyone? *Not with people I don't know. I wouldn't let bad people ride my bike.* What do bad people do? *They hit you. Friends hit you too, but only when you're fighting.* How do you make a friend? *You say, "Hi, what's your name," and that's all.*

2 (eight years old). Who's your best friend? *Shelly.* Why is Shelly your best friend? *Because she helps me when I'm getting beaten up, she cheers me when I'm sad, and she shares. . . .* What makes Shelly so special? *I've known her longer, I sit next to her and got to know her better. . . .* How come you like Shelly better than anyone else? *She's done the most for me. She never disagrees, she never eats in front of me, she never walks away when I'm crying, and she helps me on my homework. . . .* How do you get someone to like you? *Be nice and you'll get niceness in return. Really mean people*

don't deserve anything. . . . If you're nice to [your friends], they'll be nice to you.

3 (eleven years old). Who's your best friend? *Carol, but she lives far away.* Why is Carol your best friend? *She's not snobby or bratty, so we like to play together.* Could you and Carol ever stop being friends? *Maybe, but we don't let silly little things break up our friendship.* Do you have a best friend around here? *Yes, Cheryl.* Why is Cheryl your best friend? *Because I see her a lot and play with her after school.* What is a good friend like? *A person who's not snobby and plays what you want to play. Someone who does what both of you want to do. Cheryl is good to talk to and good to play with, and most of my other friends don't live near here and I can't hang around with them after school. . . .* How would you know which people to get to be your friends? *I'd spend a little time with them, get to know them, and if they were snotty or bratty I'd dump them. . . .* What do good friends do? *They help you with your problems, they help you meet new people, they play with you, they stay with you, and they do lots of things. Someone who plays with you, talks to you, hangs around with you, likes to have fun, do activities, go on picnics, and join organizations like Girl Scouts.*[19]

In the first example, the child associates friendship with playing and sharing toys. The initial bond is geographical and proximal: the friend went to the same preschool, rode the same bus, and so on. The friendship is considered as a series of momentary play encounters, and acts like hitting are not seen as having the permanent consequence of terminating the relationship. The older child in the second example still acknowledges the importance of physical contiguity ("I sit next to her. . . ."), but focuses more on the expectation that friends will assist one another in all possible ways. This child sees friendship as a relationship that strengthens over time ("I've known her longer. . . ."). Finally, the eleven-year-old in example 3 becomes selective about her choice of friends. Snobby and bratty kids are excluded: friends are those with whom one can share problems, conversation, activities, and so on. Further, friends are expected to "stay with you." The relationship now is stable as well as intimate. The reciprocity that is always at the heart of friendship is now seen as an exchange of help and confidence rather than as a mere exchange of favors (Example 2) or of play and toys (Example 1).

By early adolescence, therefore, the norm of creating friendships through simple contiguous associations is fast vanishing. So is the norm of vacillating treatment, and the norm of momentary, short-lived relationships. The abandonments of these norms go hand in hand, since friendships based on conscious choices and careful treatment are likely to last longer; and the goal of having long-lasting relations drives the desire to make careful choices about whom to have them with as well as the desire to treat friends with unremitting care.

Adolescents who treat relationships as so "plastic" that they can withstand extreme temper and abuse soon find themselves without any permanent friends. Similarly, adolescents who do not find particularly compatible people with whom to share their innermost doubts and secrets miss the rewards of intimate friendship. (And intimate self-disclosure has long been viewed as a cornerstone of mental health). In these and other ways, certain childhood standards must give way to new ones.

But all childhood standards play their part, either as a platform for further development or as a time-limited system of norms perfectly adapted to children's own culture. The usefulness of friendships based on simple association, conducted with wide behavioral fluctuation, in enabling children to have an early social life is a good example of this. Children often are thrown together for accidental reasons beyond their control. Parents move, schools organize classrooms, summer camps and other activities come and go. Children must cope with fluidity in their social life and must be able to develop quick friendships with those who pop up in their lives. Similarly, they must be able to tolerate inconsistency in how their child playmates will treat them. So these childhood friendship norms, however ill-adapted they may later become, play a critical role in maintaining the child's early social life.

Davies quotes the sociologist George Homans in describing the norm that children must live by in their friendships: "You can get to like some pretty queer customers if you go around with them long enough. The queerness becomes irrelevant." [20] In fact (and in the spirit that Homans originally intended it), this adage would not be a bad standard for regulating some difficult adult social relations as well! But even when life changes and more fortuitous interpersonal circumstances have made this norm irrelevant, we still conclude that it has served its developmental purposes.

Childhood friendships create fertile contexts for the discovery and practice of important moral standards. In large part, this is because children's friendships are eagerly initiated, closely intimate, and intensely affective in tone. In addition, childhood friend-ships are almost always more or less equal in status, especially when compared with relations between adults and children.

The orientation of children's friendships towards equality is the reason that these relationships legitimately can be called *peer* rela-tions—the modifier "peer" signifying that the parties engaged in them consider each other to have equal rights and prerogatives. Although this may sound to us like a fairly routine state of affairs, for a young child the whiff of genuine relational equality can be a somewhat unusual and delightful experience.

The very fact of "peerness" in a child's friendship enables the relationship to make a unique contribution to the child's moral growth. When child and adult interact, the child's actions and re-actions ultimately are governed by the adult's directives. In con-trast, peer friendships do not normally assume the authority of one party. Where leadership exists in a peer friendship, it is usually assigned on a very limited basis—confined, perhaps, to areas where one party has special skills. Between friends, a sense of equality predominates over the leadership of either party. This sense of equality sets the stage for a free give and take of directives and responses between the parties.

In relations founded on direct reciprocity, all parties have a shared respect for one another's equal prerogatives and perspec-tives. Accordingly, any decisions about rules of conduct within the relationship must be arrived at through consensual agreement. This orientation—which Piaget called "mutual respect"—engenders in the child a particular kind of attitude towards moral rules and obligations. The child now realizes that moral rules can be arrived at through freely chosen actions and can be adjusted by consensus to serve human needs.

Once the child has experienced rules and obligations in a rela-tionship of mutual respect, the child sees them on a more human scale. The child becomes aware that rules need not be "handed down from above" by an unimpeachable authority. Rather, rules can be created, and even changed, by people operating as equals. What makes rules "moral" or "just" is the fairness of their applica-tion to all parties and not their source in some unimpeachable ex-ternal authority. This can, and inevitably will, be tested through the collision of peer viewpoints whenever conflicts over the rule arise.

Eventually the child comes to see rules as cooperative agreements that are helpful in regulating all kinds of human interactions. This understanding, of course, favors the likelihood that the child will comply with rules, since the child recognizes their importance. The child now has a view of rules from "within"—that is, from the perspective of one who can make, alter, and enforce rules as well as one who is simply expected to follow them. This more mature perspective places the child emotionally in support of the obligation to respect social rules.

Often the child's first occasion for experiencing this "mutual" orientation towards rules is in the realm of sports and games. Here children quickly learn that rules, when equally and fairly applied, benefit everyone by enabling the game to be played with reasonable orderliness. In games, children also learn to cooperate with one another in carrying out the rules. This might mean arguing about an interpretation of a rule in a sticky situation, agreeing to change a rule where it is to everyone's advantage, or introducing a new rule if needed. Such "discussions" can be contentious and painfully loud. But in these negotiations between equals, children acquire a deep understanding and respect for the process of social regulation through rules.

One of the landmark studies in moral development was Piaget's exploration of marble games in Geneva almost sixty years ago.[21] Piaget believed that children's attitudes towards the "rules of the game" were very much at the heart of early morality. He observed children's rule-following behavior during a common Genevan street game of marbles, and asked the children what the rules meant to them. He found that young children around the age of five regard rules as permanent and sacred, not subject to modification for any reason. Piaget called this a "heteronomous" belief in rules because it entails an uncategorical subjection of oneself to laws deemed external to self.

Associated with heteronomous thinking in childhood are various forms of "moral realism." One such form is called "objective responsibility," or valuing the letter of the law above the human need for the law. An example of moral realism through objective responsibility would be saying it is wrong to ignore a "keep off the grass" sign in order to prevent a dog from digging a hole in the grass.

In his interviews with young children, Piaget found a number of anomalies of this sort. The most well-known of these was the response, given by many five-year-olds, that breaking fifteen cups clumsily while trying to help was naughtier than breaking one cup while trying to steal some jam. Piaget pointed out that such responses are examples of objective responsibility because they place the consequences of an act above the intention behind it.

Another manifestation of moral realism is "immanent justice." This is the expectation that punishment will inevitably follow a wrongdoing. Sometimes it is an act of God or nature that is expected. For example, a child might say that a boy who successfully deceives his parents with a lie will be hit by a falling branch when he goes outside. The child assumes that, like the law of gravity, moral rules are immutable aspects of the world we live in, with inevitable and unavoidable consequences on this earth.

All forms of heteronomous moral thinking arise naturally within relationships based upon authority. In authority-based relationships, rules and other constraints are indeed "handed down from above." Moreover, relations based on authority project an infallibility and inevitability about their moral prescriptions. For these reasons, Piaget theorized that heteronomous morality was a product of the adult-child relation, deriving from the "unilateral respect" that children feel for adults. Autonomous morality, on the other hand, derives from the mutual respect experienced in children's peer relations.

During early childhood, heteronomous and autonomous morality exist simultaneously. This is because young children have both adult and peer relations. But in early childhood heteronomy dominates autonomy because the parent-child relation is so overpowering. As children devote more of their social energies to peer engagements, autonomous morality waxes. In Piaget's Genevan observations, this occurred at about age eight or nine. Interestingly, Piaget reported that with this change develops a stronger tendency to obey rules consistently. The paradox is that as children begin viewing rules as less sacred and less "untouchable," they follow the rules with greater regularity. The spirit of the law seems a better guide than the letter of the law for children's prosocial conduct.

Piaget's "two social worlds of the child"—one of adult and one of peer relations[22]—complement each other in their effects on children's moral development. Peer relations have a special link to the development of moral reciprocity, kindness, cooperation, and a sense of justice. Relationships with adults, on the other hand, serve the necessary function of transmitting respect for the social order and knowledge of important social conventions. Both are essential for a well-rounded and mature sense of morality. The child needs to acquire both the outcomes and the processes that spring from each relationship. The "outcomes" are the moral principles that provide the basic building blocks for the child's moral values. The "processes" are the interactional procedures that provide the child with methods of engaging with others in a civilized manner as well as means for further enhancing the child's moral awareness.

As for outcomes, the peer relation generates equality, cooperation, kindness, and fairness. The adult-child relation generates knowledge of the social order, prescribed social rules, and the moral rationales behind them. As for processes, peer relations expose the child to interactional procedures such as direct reciprocity and consensual negotiation. Once the child learns to use these procedures, the child will become able to work out moral rules democratically with others all through life. The adult-child relation, in contrast, exposes the child to relations of authority. The child learns means of determining whether authority is morally legitimate or not. Further, the child learns respect for established rules and conventions; and, most importantly, learns respect for the social order from which all rules and social conventions arise. This, too, is a lifelong legacy, for it will enable the child to become a full citizen in society, with all of a citizen's leadership prerogatives and followership responsibilities.

In a series of studies, Youniss interviewed children about their views of child-child versus child-adult relations.[23] These interviews show that children believe that being "kind" to a peer has a very different meaning than being "kind" to an adult. In a peer relation, kindness means acting prosocially, such as helping or sharing. In a relation with adults, on the other hand, kindness means "cooperating" in a *subservient* sense, in particular obeying the adult without undue fuss.

Despite this initial contrast between peer and adult-child relations, children's experiences in peer relations bear later consequences for their relations with adults by transforming the nature of these relations. Once children learn the direct reciprocity procedures of the peer relation they begin to apply them to their adult-child relations as well. This happens toward the end of childhood or at the beginning of adolescence, when children begin conceiving of themselves as equal participants in authority-based relations, creating a greater sense of equal participation between parent and child.[24]

Furthermore, the contrast between peer and adult-induced morality may be blurred around the edges, because adults can act as friends and peers can act as authority figures. And there are many shades of gray between different patterns of relational equality, mutuality, reciprocity, and authority. As we have seen in Chapter 4, for example, some authority relations clearly favor democratic procedures more than others. But despite these many gray areas, the contrast remains valid and helpful in identifying how these two universal social relations of childhood, each in its own way, helps shape the child's emerging morality.

Because peers are close to one another in age and social status, they tend to have similar problems, wishes, and enjoyments. From an early age children communicate directly with one another about such matters.[25] Because children have so much in common with their peers, and because they talk frequently with one another about their thoughts and experiences, it is natural and relatively easy for them to share each other's perspectives. The sharing of perspectives between persons has been called "role taking" or "perspective taking." It means mentally placing oneself in another's position. In everyday terms, it is referred to as "putting yourself in the other guy's shoes."

Perspective taking is clearly a critical component of social and moral judgment. There are vigorous debates, however, about how difficult it is for one person accurately to take another's perspective. Stemming from these debates are questions about whether very young children are capable of perspective taking at all; and about how children come to understand perspectives that are radically different from their own.

It was the social philosopher George Herbert Mead who first elaborated a theory of role taking and its importance for children's moral development.[26] Mead wrote that children learn to take the role of the other through continual interaction with the social world. In the course of such interaction, they discover that their own words and gestures must mean the same thing to others if communication is to take place. Otherwise the message that one intends may be misinterpreted by others.

In conversation, therefore, two parties must monitor each other's responses and anticipate each other's thoughts. In this way, the parties can adjust their gestures and words to make sure that they are properly understood. Mead wrote that this process of "mutual adjustment" creates the role taking that is at the heart of all human discourse.

Because role taking plays such an essential role in human social life, Mead saw it developing early, perhaps by the end of infancy. Young children, he wrote, are capable of taking the role of particular others with whom they come in contact. Through specific events and actions, they get to know the attitudes and mannerisms of many individual persons.

As they grow older, children become able to take the role not just of individuals but also of the "generalized other." This means that they can infer the collective perspective of the social group to which they belong, as distinct from the particular perspective of each member. Initially this may happen on the playground, as children engage in games with many roles (pitcher and catcher, teammate and opponent). Children abstract the rules and standards of the social group by mentally assuming multiple roles in these situations. In the process of such generalized role taking, therefore, children gain an inside view of societal procedures and beliefs. This is why Mead saw role taking as central to a child's moral development.

Since Mead's time, a large body of work in developmental psychology has focused on children's role-taking abilities. A host of experimental studies have been devoted to the questions of how children learn to take other perspectives and how this capacity contributes to children's social and moral growth. Generally these experimental studies place a child with a real or imaginary peer and ask the child to reconstruct the peer's point of view. Some of the studies go further and test the hypothesis that a particular level of role-taking skill is necessary for certain kinds of moral judgment or behavior.

John Flavell and his colleagues have identified through clever experimentation the types of obstacles young children encounter when trying to take other people's perspectives.[27] Flavell believes that the greatest shortcoming of Mead's theory is that it does not pay sufficient attention to these obstacles. The major obstacle is what Flavell calls "perspective discrepancies."

People's points of view are often widely discrepant, for a number of reasons. People have different information, ideas, emotional reactions, and interests (in the broad sense) from one another. Life conditions vary widely. A wealthy person will have different needs and views than a poor one; just as an older person will have a different outlook than a younger one. A child cannot infer another's perspective correctly by a simple projection of her own. Initially, however, children do make this error, and many others as well.

When asked to tell a story from the viewpoints of three separate characters (each of whom is pictured for the subject), young children tell the identical story three times. By age six or so, many children can vary the story a bit for each telling, but often these variations lead to narrative contradictions that the children cannot resolve. Only by late childhood do children distinguish story perspectives and then weave them together into one coherent tale.

The simplest perspective problem is recognizing the very possibility of a viewpoint distinct from one's own. Yet many two-year-olds, when shown a two-sided card with a dog on the front and a cat on the back, do not realize that when they are looking at the dog someone on the other side of the card will see the cat. This difficulty in coping with perspective discrepancies can impede children's attempts to communicate in a helpful way with others. Flavell found that school-aged children often were frustrated in their attempts to help guide a blindfolded peer. They were unable to give the kinds of explicit, action-oriented messages needed by the sightless.

Robert Selman has charted the growth of children's role-taking abilities, and has outlined four childhood stages of perspective taking [28] These stages, which develop in sequence, are summarized in Table 5.1.

At Stage 0, children recognize other people's thoughts and feelings, but tend to confuse the other's mental states with their own. Our Chapter 2 example of a two-year-old offering his own security blanket to an unhappy adult is a good example of Stage 0 perspective taking. At Stage 1 children know that people have their own thoughts and feelings, but children do not understand the relation between different people's perspectives. This difficulty is demonstrated by the story-telling task described above. At Stage 2 children are able to anticipate others' perspectives and to relate them to one another (and to their own). With this ability children know how to influence others and how others may influence them. This enables them to operate very successfully within a peer dialogue.

But it is not until Stage 3 that they are able to step outside the boundaries of an interpersonal relation to assume a "third-person"

TABLE 5.1 Robert Selman's Developmental Stages
of Perspective Taking

Stage	Age range*	Child's understanding
Stage 0 Egocentric Viewpoint	3–6 yrs.	Child has a sense of differentiation of self and other but fails to distinguish between the social perspective (thoughts, feelings) of other and self. Child can label other's overt feelings but does not see the cause and effect relation of reasons to social actions.
Stage 1 Social-Informational Role Taking	6–8 yrs.	Child is aware that other has a social perspective based on other's own reasoning, which may or may not be similar to child's. However, child tends to focus on one perspective rather than coordinating viewpoints.
Stage 2 Self-Reflective Role Taking	8–10 yrs.	Child is conscious that each individual is aware of the other's perspective and that this awareness influences self and other's view of each other. Putting self in other's place is a way of judging his intentions, purposes, and actions. Child can form a coordinated chain of perspectives, but cannot yet abstract from this process to the level of simultaneous mutuality.

(Cont.)

TABLE 5.1 (Cont.)

Stage	Age range*	Child's understanding
Stage 3 Mutual Role Taking	10–12 yrs.	Child realizes that both self and other can view each other mutually and simultaneously as subjects. Child can step outside the two-person dyad and view the interaction from a third-person perspective.
Stage 4 Social and Conventional System Role Taking	12–15 + yrs.	Person realizes mutual perspective taking does not always lead to complete understanding. Social conventions are seen as necessary because they are understood by all members of the group (the generalized other) regardless of their position, role, or experience.

*Age ranges for all stages represent only an average approximation based on our studies to date.

SOURCE: Based on R. L. Selman, Social-cognitive understanding: A guide to educational and clinical practice. In T. Lickona (Ed.), *Moral Development and Behavior: Theory, Research, and Social Issues*. New York: Holt, Rinehart, & Winston, 1976, p. 309. Reprinted with permission.

perspective. This is what Mead referred to as "taking the role of the generalized other." Children at this level can evaluate a social event by standards external to the event's participants. For example, a child might decline a younger child's offer to trade a dollar of the latter's allowance for the former's piece of bubble gum on the grounds that this would be taking unfair advantage of the other.

These perspective-taking levels set the stage for children's moral judgments. Stage 1 enables children to realize that another person feels distress and may need help. Stage 2 enables a child to tailor that help to the person's specific needs and desires. It also enables children to manage some interpersonal requirements of friendships. For example, the notion of reciprocal trust in a relationship depends on the understanding that one's own actions and commitments influence the other's willingness to take similar actions and commitments, and vice versa. This understanding is made possible by Stage 2 perspective taking.

One of the premier moral notions of Western civilization is the Golden Rule, "Do unto others as you would have them do unto you." For centuries this maxim has provided people with an impetus towards altruistic actions. Prior to Stage 3 perspective taking, children interpret this notion as meaning "Do to others as they do to you." They say, in remarkably unChristlike fashion, that the Golden Rule tells us to hit back when another child hits first. At Stage 3 they are able to understand the idea that actions within a relationship can be transcended by an external standard. They also become able to take the role of a hypothetical other (as you *would have* them do . . .) in order to establish this external standard. Thus Stage 3 perspective taking makes possible the full understanding of advanced moral concepts like the Golden Rule.

Despite considerable data from the role-taking experiments of Flavell, Selman, and several others, many psychologists dispute the idea that young children fail totally to take other people's perspectives. They cite anecdotal evidence of children's empathic capacities, as discussed in Chapter 2; and draw from observations of caregiver-infant interactions, where it seems clear that even very young infants are attuned to their caregiver's moods and intentions. Some psychologists have devised ways of directly demonstrating early role-taking skill. Helen Borke, for example, simplified the task demands of perspective-taking tasks enough to enable preschoolers to assume others' viewpoints with perfect ease and competence.[29]

It is clear from this and other evidence that, under some circumstances, even infants are aware of perspectives other than their own. Certainly preschoolers can be remarkably astute about others' communication needs: one researcher showed how four-year-olds skillfully vary their linguistic patterns when called on to assist barely verbal toddlers. How, then, do we reconcile this apparent facility with research showing that perspective taking is a skill that develops over years of childhood?

The current consensus is that role taking is a multifaceted enterprise rather than one generalized ability. Some relationships and situations make taking another's role relatively simple, whereas others pose complex obstacles. A child who looks socially perceptive when discussing an intimate friend's problems may look naive when faced with a manipulative stranger.

The controversies around this issue have arisen because writers focusing on young children's role-taking difficulties often have de-emphasized children's positive capabilities. This problem stems back to Piaget, who in his early writings characterized the entire early childhood period as "egocentric." When Piaget realized that scholars interpreted this label to mean that young children are totally confined to their own perspectives, he ultimately dropped it.[30] In his own work, Piaget was moving towards a much more positive and action-based view of children's capacities: he would soon describe children's perspective-taking failures only in the context of what they knew and were able to do on specific cognitive tasks rather than as a general characteristic of early thinking. But many developmentalists have persisted in describing children's perspective taking as a unitary, general ability totally missing in all parts of young child's repertoire.

Contemporary theory and research tell us that children are born *both* sociocentric and egocentric. They are aware of others and actively seek interactive and communicative exchanges with them. If they were not to some degree always open to others' perspectives, there would be no possibility of social development. But they have much to learn about the mental states of self and other, as well as about the relation between the two.

Through social experience, especially in peer relations, children acquire more information and greater understanding of these matters. Their perspective-taking skills flourish, and they become more effective in social discourse and in their social relations generally. Perspective taking is a powerful capacity. It affects the depth of a child's moral awareness as well as the astuteness of the child's moral judgments. As the perspective-taking capacity waxes during the childhood years, children are able to act more effectively on their moral insights, thus helping others in more realistic ways.

Perspective taking, however, does not carry with it any moral imperative. It is a powerful social and intellectual tool; but it is a morally neutral one. Children always have the choice of applying their new powers of understanding others' intentions for bad as well as for good purposes. They can, for example, use their insights into another's perspective for deceitful and self-serving ends, such as adeptly tricking or cheating someone. On the other hand, if they so choose, they can use this new interpersonal awareness to pursue the altruistic goal of improving the well-being of others. It is this kind of choice that will determine the moral complexion of the child's perspective-taking acts. Such moral choices, of course, follow directly from the kinds of moral values that childen acquire throughout the course of their early development. As we have seen, influences on the child that determine what values she acquires come from within the child, from the family, and from the peer group. Beyond these, the pervasive influences of societal institutions and values play an important role as well.

6

Culture, Gender, and Morality

Moral values can be formulated in broad abstractions, but they are played out by real people in specific life situations. The people and situations all have characteristics of their own, and these incorporate the full variety of human life itself. These variations in personal and situational characteristics exert a strong influence on how morality is actualized during everyday events. There is a functional reason for this: morality always must be adaptive to the specific setting in which it functions. As a consequence, variations in human conditions across the world inevitably will lead to variations in moral thought and action.

Perhaps the oldest debate in moral philosophy is the question of whether there are any universally valid moral truths that apply across all variations in specific life settings. Are some beliefs morally right for all people in all situations everywhere, or is the validity of every moral belief dependent upon the context in which it is founded? Kant and other philosophers have suggested some universal "moral imperatives"—truth, justice, and the value of human life. Philosophers of a "relativist" persuasion, on the other hand, have argued that even these worthy "imperatives" vary in meaning, importance, and application from one situation to the next; and that in some contexts they even could lead to immoral choices.[1] Still other philosophers find neither universalism nor relativism palatable in their pure forms, and so have chosen one or another middle-ground position between the two.[2]

As we explore human variation in the moral domain, we shall repeatedly encounter this schism between the universalists and the relativists. I shall not attempt to resolve this schism here, partly because I find certain elements of each position compelling and partly because I believe that the tension between the two may be a necessary condition of moral action. For everyday moral choice inevitably must be forged from an undetermined mix of principle and practicality: even the most mundane moral act requires a creative application of moral values to an always-unique life situation. In the process, universal and contextual forces come into constant interplay, as a person struggles to find specific everyday solutions to moral concerns that usually are general to the human condition.

Both culture and gender are variations that shape children's social experience in ways that influence their moral values. Gender makes a difference for children's morality because boys and girls often are treated in different ways when they are very young. This is especially true in societies where boys and girls are prepared for entirely separate occupational roles. Such differences in treatment can result in quite distinct moral orientations, at least while children are still young. Culture makes a difference because there is wide discrepancy in the values communicated to young people in societies across the world. Because values are inevitably mediated through social communication, cultural discrepancies will lead to variations in children's moral orientations. This is true both of broad cross-cultural distinctions in moral beliefs as well as within-culture variations between the norms and values of different genders, subgroups, and so on.

In most societies throughout human history, women have taken primary responsibility for the care of the young. This means that boys and girls both experience their initial major social relationship with a female. For girls, this is a relationship with a member of the same sex; for boys, it is with a member of the opposite sex. It is just this kind of difference in social experience that can produce differences in children's moral orientations. One critical distinction in children's moral orientations—what Carol Gilligan terms an inclination towards "care" versus an inclination towards "justice"—is attributed to this gender-linked difference in children's initial social experiences with their caretakers.[3] In early childhood, girls often gravitate towards the morality of care, whereas boys often gravitate towards the morality of justice. Ultimately, Gilligan notes, males and females alike can develop an awareness of both care and justice; but because of widespread patterns of early experience, girls often orient more towards the former and boys towards the latter.

The morality of care assumes that the welfare of others is intrinsically connected to one's own welfare. People share in each other's fortunes and misfortunes and must accept responsibility for one another's well-being. This implies empathizing with another's distress and actively offering support and aid. Care and responsibility, therefore, go hand in hand.

In contrast, the morality of justice assumes that people's interests and prerogatives often conflict. What I want and deserve is not always identical to or compatible with what you want and deserve: in fact, our claims may be mutually exclusive. Formal procedures may be needed to adjudicate the conflicting claims. One such procedure is a rule of justice. By creating and maintaining such rules, people can conduct their affairs peacefully, within a system that they agree to be fair, even when they have competing self-interests.

Empirically, young girls often acquire a morality of care because from infancy on they orient towards attachment and "connectedness" with others. Boys on the other hand often orient towards individualism and "separateness" from others.

How does this empirical gender difference in moral orientation arise during development? According to recent feminist revisions of psychoanalytic theory, such differences are formed early, and irreversibly, within the mother-child relation.[4] Because boys experience their closest initial relationship with an opposite-sex parent and girls experience it with a same-sex parent, boys discover who they are through drawing contrasts between self and mother, whereas girls discover themselves by noting similarities. Gender is one of the first manifestations of a children's self-identity.[5]

As a result of these contrasting patterns of self-discovery, boys develop the notion that they are essentially different from significant others in their lives, whereas girls develop a belief in similarity and connectedness between themselves and others. As early as age three, this fundamental difference can influence the direction of boys' and girls' relations with others: "Girls emerge with a stronger basis for experiencing another's feelings as one's own . . ."[6] Boys, on the other hand, tend towards a "more emphatic individuation" which remains predominant over "their primary love and sense of empathic tie."[7] This accounts for why women tend to assume that people fundamentally have common self-interests while men tend to assume that the self-interests of individuals usually collide with one another.

Formal rules of conduct are deemed necessary when one's primary focus is on potential conflict. If one's focus is on the set of interests and needs that people share, rules and other constraints are seen as less important. The reason that men emphasize rules and fairness is that males acquire an orientation of separateness during their development. Socialized living within this orientation requires an intricate moral system that creates artificial links between persons. An orientation towards connectedness, in contrast, requires no such system of formal rules. Rather, what is needed is a sensitivity towards the needs of others, a spirit of benevolence, and a determination to conduct one's affairs accordingly. These are the qualities that are instrumental in the "morality of care"—a morality that typifies the orientations of many women in contemporary society.[8]

In order to illustrate how such gender differences can influence children's moral sensibilities, Gilligan has quoted examples of boys' and girls' reasoning on moral dilemmas. In one case, eleven-year-old Amy is set against same-aged Jake. In the following example, Amy sees the moral dilemma as a "narrative of relationships that extends over time," whereas Jake sees it as a "math problem with humans."[9]

In this classic dilemma designed by Lawrence Kohlberg, an early pioneer in the study of moral development, a man is desperate to save his wife, who is dying of cancer. A cure is available in the form of a drug, but the druggist who controls the drug charges more money for it than the man has. Should the man steal the drug? Amy and Jake respond in the following manners:

> *Amy:* Well I don't think so. I think there might be other ways besides stealing it, like if he could borrow the money or make a loan or something, but he really shouldn't steal the drug—but his wife shouldn't die either. If he stole the drug, he might save his wife then, but if he did, he might have to go to jail, and then his wife might get sicker again, and he couldn't get any more of the drug, and it might not be good. So, they should really just talk it out and find some other ways to make the money.

> *Jake* (explaining his answer that the man, Heinz, should steal the drug): For one thing, a human life is worth more than money, and if the druggist only makes a thousand dollars, he is still going to live, but if Heinz doesn't steal the drug, his wife is going to die. (*Why is a life worth more than money?*) Because the druggist can get a thousand dollars later from rich people with cancer, but Heinz can't get his wife again. (*Why*

not?) Because people are all different and so you couldn't get Heinz's wife again.[10]

In these examples, Amy's assumption that people can work out their problems by "talking it out" is contrasted with Jake's sense that people sometimes must act on their own, even in opposition to others, if they are to do the right thing.

Because Amy sees the social world as a network of relationships, she believes that the solution to the problem lies in making the wife's condition evident to everyone concerned, especially the druggist. Surely then all the people in the situation will work something out to respond to the wife's needs. Jake, on the other hand, assumes no such ultimate concordance among the story's characters. As a consequence, Jake believes that Heinz may need to take the law into his own hands if he is to protect his rights. Jake concludes that the wife's life is indeed a legitimate part of Heinz's rights by performing a logical calculation establishing the unique value of the wife's life.

In order to capture the special properties of female moral development, Gilligan has proposed a new sequence of stages based upon the morality of care and relationships.[11] This sequence for female moral development has three levels, or "moral perspectives." The first level is an ethic of "caring for the self in order to ensure survival." This is rejected as being "selfish" during the girl's subsequent transition to the next level's "maternal" ethic that assumes responsibility for others' welfare and values care and responsibility for others. The transition beyond this phase comes when one realizes that the self as well as others requires care. The third and final perspective redresses the earlier unbalanced sacrifice of self "through a new understanding of the interconnection between other and self." This new sense of self-other interdependence enables one to separate out the self's needs where appropriate. Thus at the final level "the activity of care enhances both other and self."

Consistent with Gilligan's writings on female moral judgment, Nancy Eisenberg and her colleagues found that, by age eleven or twelve, boys and girls tend to diverge in their sympathetic and role-taking reasoning, with girls emphasizing many of the concerns described by Gilligan.[12] Observations of children's play have further documented some of the gender differences mentioned above. Piaget long ago found that boys, unlike girls, tend towards organized games with elaborate rules.[13] Like lawyers-in-training, many boys are fascinated with game procedures in and of themselves, and delight in creating and negotiating complex systems of formal rules. Girls often prefer dyadic or small-group play, such as informal turn-taking games with few participants. But it must be noted that these are normative differences between the gender groups as a whole. Many individual boys and girls do just the opposite and thrive developmentally.

There is also a generalized difference between boys and girls in their tendencies towards aggression and empathy. Even at a very young age, boys favor aggressive, "rough-and-tumble" play, whereas girls often shy away from hard physical contact.[14] There may be hormonal and other physiological factors that support this gender difference in early play preference. In addition, girls seem more inclined than boys towards empathic responses—at least on some measures of empathy—and also more inclined towards altruistic acts than boys.[15] (Again, the gender groups overlap on these dimensions, so that some girls are more aggressive than many boys, and some boys are more empathic than many girls.[16]) Further, boys have a stronger inclincation than girls to perform altruistic acts consonant with the male image—such as carrying parcels, protecting siblings, or helping the elderly cross the street.[17]

The great unanswered question about such generalized gender differences is: How linked are they to changeable patterns of socialization? As women enter into societal roles similar to those traditionally held by men, will they tend to be more like men in moral orientation? Or will inevitable realities of mother-child relations (such as the unavoidable mother-daughter similarity and mother-son contrast) make these gender differences endure as long as mothers remain the primary caretakers of children? This is a critical question for future generations. Its final answer will determine the limits of social change.

We have some good reasons to believe that gender differences in moral orientation can quickly vanish under new social circumstances. (This should not be surprising, since gender patterns of moral orientation arise in the first place through the differential social experience of boys and girls.) We know that when women enter occupations that have been traditionally reserved for men, their moral orientations broaden to incorporate the elements of justice reasoning associated with male morality. Female lawyers are as developed in reasoning about justice and rights as are male lawyers. Studies have shown that men and women with similar occupational histories score essentially identically on tests of moral judgment.[18] Although the evidence on this is still somewhat mixed, generally it is when women working in traditionally female household roles are compared with men working in traditionally male occupational roles that we find the most striking differences of the sort described above.

Moreover, we know that cultural differences can exaggerate gender differences in children's moral orientations. Anthropologists have reported that contrasts between boys' and girls' values are far sharper in traditional cultures than in Western technological societies. Girls in agrarian parts of Africa and Asia tend to be much more nuturant and cooperative than boys in those cultures.[19] While the same *direction* of difference can be observed between boys and girls in the West, the *extent* of the contrast is much less striking, with great overlap between the two genders on these dimensions.

This cultural difference may reflect differences between parental expectations in agrarian and Western societies. In many African and Asian communities parents expect daughters to spend much of their time helping with the care of younger siblings. They do not expect sons to do so. In the West, there is some of this difference—for example, girls do more babysitting. But generally Western girls and boys alike spend their time either in school or playing with peers, rather than helping mothers rear the young. In countries where the traditional culture has become increasingly "Westernized," parental expectations for daughters have changed, and the gap between girls' and boys' moral orientations has diminished.[20]

So social change, if it leads to greater equality between the sexes and to greater similarity in their societal roles, may make the gender differences in moral orientation anachronistic. But it would be a mistake to see such change, if it occurs, as merely a product of blind social forces. Vast issues of ideology are at stake. The controversies are consciously created and recognized; and the choices, at least to some extent, are under human control. The ideological choice is whether to value or devalue the very *fact* of ethical difference between the sexes. There is no question that we should value the moral orientations—justice and care—associated with each sex, but there is a serious question as to whether we should value the moral separation that the association with gender signifies.

The appeal of Gilligan's writings on the morality of care has been the value that she has found in an often-neglected area of moral concern. The possibility that the morality of care represents female more than male morality enhances that appeal, since it suggests that such concerns have been neglected precisely because women have been relatively powerless in society. Gilligan's *tour de force* was in taking an orientation associated with powerlessness and treating it as a moral strength. In fact, in reading Gilligan one often comes away with the sense that, of the two moral orientations, care represents the greater virtue.

I do not dispute the relative merits of care versus justice. I would agree that care-linked virtues like charity, mercy, and forgiveness are the *sine qua non* of morality, and any social theory that underplays them is guilty of a grievous omission. But I do question the inevitability of their link with femininity as opposed to masculinity. In fact, my favorite piece of advocacy for the priority of caring values in a moral framework is expressed by a male character in a male-oriented novel written by a male author: Victor Hugo's saintly bishop in *Les Miserables* voices the following prayer:

> Oh you who are! Ecclesiastes calls you Omnipotence; the
> Maccabees call you Creator; the Epistle and the Ephesians call
> you Liberty; Baruch calls you Immensity; the Psalms call you
> Wisdom and Truth; St. John calls you Light; the Book of
> Kings calls you Lord; Exodus calls you Providence; Leviticus,
> Holiness; Esdras, Justice; Creation calls you God; man calls
> you the Father; but Solomon calls you Mercy, and that is the
> fairest of all your names.[21]

No one can dispute that men can value caring just as women can value justice. The vagaries of social experience may orient girls towards one and boys towards the other, particularly in cultural settings that establish more nurturant roles and expectations for girls. Does this difference in orientations have any social value itself? Is it worth preserving for future generations? For myself, I doubt it. The values of care and justice are by no means incompatible, and both should be fostered in every child. If this means blurring the differences between the two sexes, it is for the benefit of each. It could help weaken the gender stereotypes that have limited the opportunities of girls and have contributed to the subordination of women. It should enhance the moral awareness of boys and girls alike. By removing gender-linked constraints on children's values we may provide children with their best chance to expand their moral horizons to the full limits of human potential.

Gender can influence a child's moral orientation if and only if gender makes a difference to the child's social context, for the child's moral thinking and behavior is mediated by the child's social experience and not by gender directly. Accordingly, gender is but one of many interpersonal qualities that may influence the substance and direction of children's morality in settings where such qualities have social or cultural significance. In this light, the specific qualities themselves are secondary: the critical variables are the societal norms, values, and expectations that give all such qualities their ultimate importance. This, in fact, is what modern anthropologists mean when they say that the essence of any culture lies in its unique systems of meaning rather than any particular behavioral pattern.[22] Cultural meaning systems can and do vary radically around the world, and with them the shape of children's morality. For this reason, a comprehensive view of moral development requires us to consider cultural perspectives radically different from our own.

A case in point is the seriousness with which children living in parts of India take certain social rules that Western children would consider to be minor social conventions; and, conversely, the moral lack of interest that these Indian children show in violations that are considered grave by Western standards. Richard Shweder compared the moral conceptions of American children with those of children that he observed during field trips to India.[23] India, like many other non-Western societies, treats moral rules as part of the natural world order. This means that many Indians do not distinguish between physical, moral, and social regulation in the same manner as do Westerners. In India, for example, violations of such customs as food taboos and marital restrictions can be treated just as seriously as acts intended to cause harm to others, and can be considered as much a breach of nature as an attempt to desecrate the living human body. Social rules are considered to be inevitable, much like the law of gravity: "Forms of human association are thought to be found (natural law), not founded (conventionalism)."[24]

One of Shweder's findings demonstrates how thoroughly such cultural particularities permeate children's moral attitudes. From interviews with Indian children ages eight to ten, Shweder ranked a large number (thirty-nine) of their social and moral concerns from those considered most serious by the Indian children to those considered least serious. The last few concerns at the end of Shweder's list, for example, were not even judged to be real violations of any important norm. Table 6.1 presents a sample dozen of these concerns, presented in the order in which they appear on Shweder's larger list. The numbers in parentheses are their exact ranks out of the original thirty-nine concerns that Shweder identified.

We can see by looking at the list that these Indian children worry much more about certain food transgressions than about uncharitable behavior or domestic violence (under conditions where they deem such behavior appropriate). In addition, the propriety of women's behavior as manifested by standards of dress, cleanliness, and familial role is a very high-priority item.

American children differ significantly from their Indian counterparts in their rankings of these same concerns. The American children disapprove strongly of behaviors that Indian children judge to be "not a breach" and, conversely, they show disregard for standards that the Indian children hold dear. There is some, but not much, overlap of moral concerns between the two cultures (see Table 6.2). These data clearly establish the fundamentally different moral views of the Indian and American children in Shweder's study.

For Westerners accustomed to viewing morality as a social contract freely chosen, Indian beliefs pose a new world view—one not easy to reconcile with such treasured notions as the autonomy of individual conscience. Yet this world view is considered by many to be every bit as rational and as functional as our own, and no doubt is held by a far greater portion of humankind. It also presents similar developmental challenges to children learning to live within a culture. We cannot completely understand these challenges until we have examined the many forms they can take in diverse contexts around the world.

In Chapter 4 we saw how different child-rearing patterns can influence children's moral orientations in a variety of ways. Some child-rearing behaviors (like the use or nonuse of praise) arise from specific cultural conditions and priorities throughout the world. These parental behaviors can communicate to the child standards that in turn will ensure the continuity of the culture across generations.

In all of this contextual variety, we might wonder whether there

TABLE 6.1 Twelve Offenses, Ranked from Worst (1) to Least Bad (12) by Hindu Brahmin Children Ages 8–10. The Number on the Right Indicates Each Offense's Rank out of 39 Possible Breaches.

1. The day after his father's death, the eldest son had a haircut and ate chicken. (1)
2. A woman cooked rice and wanted to eat with her husband and his elder brother. Then she ate with them. (6)
3. Once a doctor's daughter met a garbage man, fell in love with him, and decided to marry him. The father of the girl opposed the marriage and tried to stop it, because the boy was a garbage man. In spite of the opposition from the father, the girl married the garbage man. (10)
4. A beggar was begging from house to house with his wife and sick child. A home owner drove him away without giving him anything. (12)
5. In a family, a 25-year-old addresses his father by his first name. (13)
6. A poor man went to the hospital after being seriously hurt in an accident. At the hospital they refused to treat him because he could not afford to pay. (15)
7. A woman is playing cards at home with her friends. Her husband is cooking rice for them. (18)
8. A father told his son to steal flowers from his neighbor's garden. The boy did it. (19)
9. Two people applied for a job. One of them was a relative of the interviewer. Because they were relatives, he was given the job although the other man did better on the exam. (21)
10. A letter arrived addressed to a 14-year-old son. Before the boy returned home, his father opened the letter and read it. (34)
11. A young married woman went alone to see a movie without informing her husband. When she returned home, her husband said, "If you do it again, I will beat you black and blue." She did it again; he beat her black and blue. (35)
12. A boy played hookey from school. The teacher told the boy's father and the father warned the boy not to do it again. But the boy did it again and the father beat him with a cane. (37)

SOURCE: Adapted from R. Schweder, M. Mahapatra, and J. Miller (1987) Culture and moral development. In J. Kagan and S. Lamb (Eds.) *The Emergence of Morality in Young Children.* Chicago: University of Chicago Press.

is any core aspect of moral development that transcends the vagaries of time and place. Is there a set of principles that civilized people everywhere recognize as morally necessary? Or, if not principles, is there a moral process of some other sort that applies

TABLE 6.2 Patterns of Agreement and Disagreement Between American and Hindu Brahmin Children about What is Right and What is Wrong.

Disagreement: Brahmin children think it is right, American children think it is wrong.

Caning an errant child
Eating with hands
Father opening son's letter

Disagreement: Brahmin children think it is wrong, American children think it is right.

Addressing father by first name
Eating beef
Cooking in clothes worn while (earlier) defecating
Cutting hair and eating chicken after father's death

Agreement: American and Brahmin children think it is wrong.

Ignoring beggar
Breaking promise
Destroying another's picture
Kicking harmless animal
Stealing flowers

Agreement: Brahmin and American children think it is right.

Men holding hands

For the remaining 26 offenses there was dissensus within one or the other community.
SOURCE: Adapted from R. Schweder, M. Mahapatra, and J. Miller (1987) Culture and moral development. In J. Kagan and S. Lamb (Eds.) *The Emergence of Morality in Young Children.* Chicago: University of Chicago Press.

generally to human life? Perhaps a universal set of emotional responses to archtypical moral events? A set of basic concerns that people find morally compelling? A sequence of moral ideas and values through which children everywhere pass in the course of their social development?

Of interest to us here are not the specifics of the relativist/universalist debate—much of which revolves around technical and definitional issues such as how one frames the "moral domain" as opposed to other social regulatory systems—but how the debate illuminates the varieties of children's morality. For in arguing through their universalist or relativistic positions, social scientists have expanded our vision of children's moral inclinations. Shweder's investigations in India and America reveal that there are sharp cultural differences in what people judge to be right and wrong. These differences can be seen in comparisons between children as well as adults in the two cultures. Many of the differences seem surprising, even shocking, to a member of one culture who is unfamiliar with the other.

That there should be some circumstances in which a man may beat his wife "black and blue," for example, is a repugnant notion to most Westerners. Shweder finds Hindu Brahmin children rating this among the lowest of their moral concerns, not considering it to be even a breach of the moral order (see Table 6.1).[25] At the other extreme, these children believe that a widow eating fish or a man having his hair cut right after his father's death are the gravest of moral violations. American children, predictably enough, strongly condemn wife beating while condoning fish eating and hair cutting under any circumstances.

There were areas of overlap between the two groups, where, for example, both thought that breaking promises and ignoring poor beggers was wrong. If further study in other cultures revealed a similar consensus around the same cases, these might be candidates for universal moral concerns. At least one item on one overlap list, incest, has been previously identified by many anthropologists as a possibly universal taboo. But Shweder takes pains to note that the agreed-upon breaches were not the ones that *either* group was most concerned about. Even if these breaches should prove universal in their appeal, they were not as compelling as the culturally specific items. (Unfortunately Shweder did not include in his inventory certain breaches that might have proven both universal and strongly compelling, such as murdering or torturing innocent persons).

Shweder suggests that the culturally specific parts of moral codes are rational and essential, even if they may seem bizarre to nonmembers of the culture. If Westerners fully understood the importance of family respect, eating prohibitions, and asymmetrical man-woman relations to Hindu Brahmin culture, the Indian children's moral priorities would seem more defensible. In this manner, Shweder suggests, it may be possible for Westerners to rationalize such behaviors as food rituals and even circumstantial physical violence between husband and wife. The key is that the entire social order is built upon assumptions that dictate the culturally specific codes in question.

Needless to say, Oriya [Hindu] Brahmins do not view beating
an errant wife as an instance of arbitrary assault. . . . [They]
believe that beating a wife who goes to the movies without
permission is roughly equivalent to corporal punishment for a
private in the army who leaves the military base without
permission. For Oriyas there are rationally appealing
analogical mappings between the family as a unit and military
units (differentiated roles and status obligations in the service
of the whole, hierarchical control, drafting and induction,
etc.). One thing the family is not, for Oriyas, is a voluntary
association among co-equal individuals.[26]

Those of us with more universalist leanings would reject such a
rationalization. We would hold that violent and sexist practices
like wife beating are morally wrong in any circumstances, whatever their cultural or historical roots. Even in the societies that
harbor such practices, there are many who speak out against them
on moral grounds. Witness, for example, the rising outcry within
India against the infamous male tradition of "bride-burning" as a
means of blackmailing one's in-laws into continual dowry pay-
ments. The debate within and without South Africa about the rac-
ist policy of apartheid can be seen in a similar light.
   Such arguments place universalists in the often uncomfortable
position of condemning practices that have been adopted by large
portions of the world for generations. Relativists, in turn, levy
charges of elitism and intolerance against those who would stand
in judgment of another society's traditional practices. But even traditional societies are not wholly united behind every cultural practice. There are always within every society critics, skeptics, and
those who push for social change. The prime minister of India,
for example, recently deplored the sexism inherent in many of his
country's traditional practices: "Women are the most disadvan-
taged and discriminated in this society. It is shame and a sign of
backwardness in our own thinking and mentality."[27] Thus universal
principles of human rights can and do arise within traditional cultures, and it is reasonable for those in any culture to applaud and
support such trends wherever they occur.
   Children, of course, rarely make such meta-cultural judgments,
since their main exposure to moral concerns comes either from
direct experience within their own culture or from communi-

cations by parents and peers, also a part of their own culture. Children learn their within-culture moral lessons quickly and well. By age five, children in both India and America have enough familiarity with their culture's codes and assumptions to generate consistent, culturally appropriate responses to moral questions. As the children grow older, the consistency and relative conformity of their responses increases even more. Adults closely share the moral affirmations and negations of their cultural compatriots. This means that, as a group, adults and children of one culture can and do differ broadly from those of another in many of their moral views.

Interestingly, Indian and American children differ even in their *direction of development* towards—or away from—a universalized application of their moral codes. In Shweder's sample, the American children were more likely than the American adults to assert that all moral standards should apply to everyone across situations. The American adults, in contrast, tended to modify the standards when faced with the complexities of real-life cases. It was as if these adults were expressing the common sentiment—traditionally passed from adult to child in our society—that ideals do not always work in the real world, and that sometimes compromises or alternative solutions are the best course.

The Indian developmental path was quite the opposite. Whereas in the American sample universal moral thinking was far more prevalent among children than among adults, in the Indian sample there was an increasing tendency with age to apply one's moral standards to all conceivable contexts. These data suggest the intriguing possibility that growing up in some cultures may mean not simply acquiring different sets of moral values, but an entirely different orientation to the moral universe. It may be that moral maturity in some parts of the world implies an ever-expanding tendency to universalize one's moral beliefs, whereas in other parts of the world moral maturity means applying one's beliefs flexibly to an array of changing situations.

American culture has been known for its pragmatic bent, and moral compromise is often seen as a part of mature realism. Its anti-idealist ethic can be summed up in a quote from a non-American novel that achieved great popularity in the West, Boris Pasternak's *Dr. Zhivago*: "And if he were really to do good, he would have needed, in addition to his principles, a heart capable of violating them—a heart which knows only of the particular, not of the general case, and which achieves greatness in little actions."[28]

It is clear that an alternative world view exists. Moral growth can be conceived as the formation of a more unified and cohesive approach to moral problems rather than as an increasing adeptness at fashioning one's moral choices to meet the particular demands of the moment. There are arguments in favor of either approach, and parts of these arguments derive from the cultural conditions that foster each.

In a culture like India's (as Schweder sees it), where culturally specific practices take on the most profound moral and religious import, the problem for a reflective person within that culture is to find the general principle behind the practice. How does this eating ritual or that marital convention contribute to the general good? The developmental task for a person aspiring to a self-examined moral awareness becomes a creative one of universalizing specific codes and practices that have been closely defined for generations.

Western moral doctrine, in contrast, tends to elevate abstract principes like justice and welfare to a higher moral status then customs and conventions. In simplified and distilled form, children quickly learn these principles in their play: witness, for example, the evidence on children's early sharing and empathic behavior discussed in Chapters 2 and 3. The problem then becomes how to apply these principles to an increasingly complex array of specific social problems, and how to coordinate these principles with other social expectations such as dress codes, rules of manners, and other social conventions and customs. This becomes an exercise in application, interpretation, and modification of one's moral ideals. Hence a different developmental path in search of an opposite kind of goal.

Recent findings from other cross-cultural research suggest that the Western tendency to separate morality from convention and custom may not be shared by the vast majority of the world's peoples. Further, socialization practices in many third world countries actively instill in children as great a respect for their culture's traditional codes and practices as for abstract moral principles like justice.

Carolyn Pope Edwards looked for "moral encounters" in recorded observations of twenty-eight Kenyan children ages seven to sixteen.[29] These children lived in a small rural community of about 250 in all. Edwards was especially interested in events that would reveal these Kenyan children's attitudes towards aggression, rules, parental commands, and local customs. The Kenyan observations reveal a social world rich in communication about proper standards of behavior. Parents instruct children and children instruct one another about do's and don'ts. Instructions are liberally sprinkled with commands, threats, and actual physical punishments. These constraining communications advance a wide variety of standards, from prohibitions against aggressions to neatness and respect for property. These social standards are consistently and vigorously enforced. Community standards of propriety seem as strenuously defended as do those of justice and welfare. In fact, there seems to be a curious ambivalence about the community standards regarding physical harm. While aggression is actively discouraged, it is also widely practiced as an enforcement and punishment technique. Young members of the culture receive, and follow, the message that beating others sometimes is an appropriate response to their transgressions.

Children as well as parents in Kenya participate in the communication and enforcement of all community standards. The children's eagerness to assume the enforcer role leaves no doubt that they have learned the standard. Whether in all cases they have fully "internalized" it is another question. In Edwards's examples, some of the young seem a bit too eager to rely on violence in their enforcement role, and they are often corrected for this by adults. No doubt as the children grow older they will learn more about the permissible standards of corporal punishment in their culture.

Edwards' Kenyan observations, like Shweder's Indian data, reveal that children in many cultures grow up with a radically different set of moral priorities than those experienced by Western children. Because these cultures treat moral rules as part of the natural world order, they do not distinguish between the various forms of social regulation in the same manner as Westerners do. Violation of cultural conventions can be as strictly discouraged as acts intended to cause harm to others, and may even be enforced by acts that appear physically harmful. Moral development within such cultures entails acquiring deep respect for the "natural" codes that one is taught as a child as well as gaining a general understanding of these codes' importance for the culture's way of life.

Mature members of the non-Western cultures place a fundamental value on social conventions because they appreciate the role of

tradition in maintaining family ties and social order. These are critical features of societies that ground themselves in the notion of
interdependence between persons rather than independence of
persons from one another. Accepting social conventions as a basic
part of the natural moral code contributes to the spirit of human
interdependence. Robert LeVine and Merry White write:

> Anthropological field workers have long reported that diverse
> non-Western peoples . . . do not make so sharp a distinction
> between the person and the group as is made in the West. . . .
> A person is punished, along with others, for a crime
> committed by another member of his or her kin group. . . . A
> young woman who is asked for her opinion on an issue refers
> the investigator to her father-in-law, the head of the family,
> rather than answering herself. . . . Those who behave in
> accordance with social convention are assumed to be
> intelligent in the way that counts the most, i.e., in their
> maintenance of the social linkages that mean long-term
> security. . . .[30]

Studies of Westerners grappling with issues of morality and social convention suggest quite a different picture.[31] Elliott Turiel
has reported that children in our society clearly distinguish moral
problems of justice and welfare from conventional problems of
dress, eating behavior, and manners (saying "please" and "thank
you", or addressing grown-ups as "Mr." and "Mrs."). Turiel found
American children as young as five distinguishing between moral
and conventional codes and holding the moral ones more important. On the playground, American children themselves enforce
moral standards (don't hit; stay away from that bike) whereas they
pay less attention to conventional infractions. American adults, on
the other hand, constantly urge children to follow conventions
(say please; pull down your shirt) whereas they often leave it to
children to work out problems of fairness and aggression between
themselves.

From the child's point of view, this dual experience with moral
and conventional codes leaves the impression that morality can be
inferred directly from one's encounters with injustice and aggression, whereas conventions must be transmitted through social
communication. Morality is part of the everyday world of childhood, whereas conventions are something that adults harp on.
This gives the child the sense that morality is the authentic means

of social regulation, whereas conventions are somewhat arbitrary and external to one's real interest. This sense endures throughout development, producing the Western manner of drawing a major (and invidious) distinction between morality and conventions.

Is this not merely a Western distinction but a sound and proper one? Turiel believes so, asserting that it is the moral rules, not the conventional ones, that provide equal protection for all people's rights. He quotes from the contemporary philosopher Dworkin in maintaining that "We cannot leave justice to convention. . . . Moral traditions are not clubs into which the peoples of the world are distributed so that everyone carries a membership card in one but only one."[32]

The debate between cultural relativism and universalism pits our wish to respect human diversity against our beliefs in values like equality, liberty, and human rights. Those who hold tolerance for diversity dearest withhold judgment about cultural patterns that foster inequality, restriction, and the curtailment of certain rights as part of their traditional social order. Such a perspective can even go so far as tolerating intolerance in other cultures. It can also in effect elevate tolerance to the status of an absolute standard—a seeming contradiction, since relativism supposedly disclaims all moral absolutes.

In contrast, those who believe that such principles as equality and human rights are absolute in a moral sense will claim these as universal standards. Consequently, they will not refrain from making judgments about any cultural practices that deviate from these standards. For my own part, I find my reactions to certain human behavior—such as the oppressive cultural practices described by Shweder—so compelling that I generally find myself leaning to the universalist position. But there are no data that can resolve this debate, and sound philosophical logic can be applied to both sides.

As I noted earlier, my conviction as a social scientist is that we must appreciate the tension between these two positions in order to understand moral action in real social settings. This is especially true of understanding moral action across diverse cultural contexts. By examining closely the unique moral beliefs that are held within particular cultures, while at the same time identifying comparable moral standards that apply between cultures, we can illuminate the parallels and variations in children's morality as it develops in diverse social conditions.

Working productively with the tension between competing

ideological positions is an exercise in scientific objectivity, and a commendable one at that. But scientific objectivity does not imply that, as educators and parents, we must maintain a neutral position between universalism and relativism. Nor does it imply a value neutrality of any sort. Enlightened moral education requires us to make full use of our social-science knowledge; but it does not require us to abandon our values. Neither does it require us to modify them, nor even to moderate them, as a gesture towards relativism, in forging an enlightened and effective approach to moral education at home and in the schools.

7

Fostering Children's Moral Growth

I begin with an assumption that I believe is widely shared: we wish to do whatever is possible to foster our children's moral growth. Moreover, I believe that most adults in our society would agree on many of the key elements of moral growth. For example, almost all adults agree that children should be honest, kind, fair, responsible, and respectful of social rules and authority. Certainly there are differences among us in how we interpret and set priorities for these virtues; and there are plenty of controversial moral issues— sex, religion, and politics, for example—that divide us. But we should not let these divisions blur our focus on our many areas of agreement. In many of our most fundamental aspirations for our children's morality, we hold similar goals and visions.

Why, then, are we not able to mobilize a unified campaign to encourage moral growth in our young? Why do we, as a society, seem almost paralyzed when faced with signs of moral apathy (and, in too many cases, outright moral degradation) in youth today? Surely our paralysis is not due to confusion or debates over our broadest goals. None of us wants to raise children who lie, cheat, steal, act cruelly towards others, or refuse to assume responsibility at home or at school. None of us wants our children to ignore adult prohibitions against drugs, drinking, reckless driving, irresponsible and risky sex, or antisocial behavior in any form. As a society with such unequivocal common goals, why do we refrain from waging "the moral equivalent of war" on the side of children's morality?

The problem is not the strength and clarity of our goals but rather the quality of our understanding. We have poor societal knowledge of children's morality and its developmental sources. The conceptions currently "at large" in the public purview consist of myths based either on religious or political biases or on obsolete psychological theorizing. The distortions that result are often further from the truth than our own common-sense intuititions, however unformulated and biased these may be. State-of-the-art social science, which could correct the distortions, rarely gets a hearing other than in cursory journalistic accounts.

Many of our popular myths about children's moral development have been around, in one form or another, for a long time. Not surprisingly, they tend to contradict one another, for they arise from distinct competing views about human nature. Here are some of the more prevalent myths that one might encounter through public discourse and media presentations:

1. Children are naturally good but become morally corrupted when exposed to the wrong social influences.

2. Children are born with predominantly immoral tendencies, and moral sensibilities must be imposed upon them against their will from the outside.

3. The parent is solely responsible for the child's moral character.

4. There is little that anyone can do about the child's moral character, since the child's personality is formed through congenital factors that are largely beyond anyone's control.

5. Children's peers are a deleterious influence on their moral judgment and conduct.

6. For the sake of their moral growth, children need to be shielded from television, film, or music performances that suggest poor moral values.

7. Moral education means telling children about the values held by our society and the virtues expected of them.

Now these notions may seem benign enough on their face. After all, they all reflect the best intentions of adults earnestly trying to preserve, protect, and encourage children's moral sensibilities. But the consequences of these notions for our efforts to morally educate children are not so benign. For one thing, they funnel our efforts into directions that are fruitless at best and counterproductive at worst. For another thing, their incompatibility with one another divides and dilutes our efforts, making effective joint action all but impossible. As a result, they prevent us from taking the direct, informed steps that could make a difference for our children's moral lives.

Let us start from a more secure and cohesive base of knowledge. We know from scientific studies and observations that children's moral development is characterized by the principles summarized below. Because these principles complement rather than clash with one another, they can be used together in a coherent and internally consistent account of moral growth. Moreover, they can set the stage for a comprehensive approach to children's moral education.

1. Simply by virtue of their participation in essential social relationships, children encounter the classic moral issues facing humans everywhere: issues of fairness, honesty, responsibility, kindness, and obedience. Moral awareness, therefore, come from "within" a child's normal social experience. It may need to be bolstered, guided, informed, and enhanced, but it does not need to be imposed from the outside.

2. The child's moral awareness is shaped and supported by natural emotional reactions to observations and events. These reactions begin as early as infancy. They can be quite intense in both positive and negative directions. There are emotional reactions like empathy that support moral compassion and prosocial action. There are also reactions like shame, guilt, and fear that support obedience and rule following. Further, children's love and attachment feelings for their parents establish an emotional foundation for children's developing respect for authority.

3. Relations with parents, teachers, and other adults introduce the child to important social standards, rules, and conventions. Moreover, these relations generate knowledge and respect for the social order itself, including its principles of organization and legitimate authority. *Authoritative* adult-child relations, in which firm demands are made of the child while at the same time there is clear communication between adult and child about the nature and justification of these demands, yield the most positive results for child's moral judgment and conduct.

4. Relations with peers introduce children to norms of direct reciprocity and to standards of sharing, cooperation, and fairness. In peer relations, children develop new procedures for interacting with others. Some of these are useful only in the social world of childhood, but others endure: in particular, the child's sense of equality and mutuality, originally fostered by engagements with

peers, ultimately transforms many of the child's other relations into more egalitarian and intimate forms. Moreover, the perspective-taking skills fostered by peer relations enhance children's growing moral awareness and improve the effectiveness of children's helping acts.

5. Because children's morality is shaped (though not wholly created) through social influence, broad variations in social experience can lead to broad differences in children's moral orientations. One such variation can be found in the different roles, expectations, and other forms of treatment to which boys and girls are exposed, particularly in more traditional social environments. This may lead to the observed tendency for girls to orient more towards the morality of care and boys towards the morality of rules and justice. Another such variation is the radically different system of social norms and values that can be found in many of the world's non-Western cultures. This can lead children from different cultures to adopt very different moral priorities. But we also have reason to believe that such orientations, which are socially generated, can be socially transformed as cultures change. In a culture freed from traditional sex roles, there is no reason why boys and girls alike cannot learn to use both the morality of care and the morality of justice with equal facility. In a similar vein, there are people from all cultures that can and do appreciate the universal moral values of truth, human rights, human welfare, and justice; and this becomes increasingly the case under conditions of social change and progress.

6. Moral growth in school settings is governed by the same developmental processes that apply to moral growth everywhere. This means that children acquire moral values by actively participating in adult-child and child-child relationships that support, enhance, and guide their natural moral inclinations. Children's morality is little affected by lessons or lectures for which they are at best passive recipients and at worst captive and recalcitrant audiences. Further, as with the rest of a child's social life, the quality of the school interactions communicates a moral message that is more enduring than any explicit statements that teachers might make. It is not feasible to train children in democratic values simply by indoctrination and verbal directives. For an adequate moral education in a democratic society, children must come to understand the open, egalitarian interactional procedures implied by democratic

values. Such understanding can be fully acquired only through frequent participation in social engagements that are founded upon such procedures.

Children's morality, therefore, is a product of affective, cognitive, and social forces that converge to create a growing moral awareness. The child begins with some natural emotional reactions to social events; these are supported, refined, and enhanced through social experience. In the course of this social experience, the child actively participates in relations with peers and adults, always observing and interpreting the resulting interactions. From this web of participation, observation, and interpretation, the child develops enduring moral values.

There are many ways for adults to enter into this process constructively; but there also are ways that are ineffectual and, still worse, counterproductive. For example, we saw in Chapter 4 the deleterious effects of "authoritarian" child-rearing patterns. We also saw similar results from a different form of parental intrusiveness, the overly protective child-rearing pattern called "permissiveness." Such mistakes are not confined to the home. Many schools also err in one or the other direction of the authoritarian or the permissive mode. In the one case, they err by enforcing their moral codes in an unresponsive and (to the child) arbitrary fashion; and in the other they err by allowing the child too often to avoid sanctions for code violation. Neither course offers the child much opportunity to develop respect for the many reasonable moral codes, consistently applied, that bind together our social universe.

If they are to contribute positively to children's moral growth, both parents and schools must operate with an awareness of the child's developmental needs. For moral growth, the primary developmental need is full participation in the kinds of social experiences that will build upon the child's nascent moral sensibilities. In order to create contexts for children's full participation and moral learning, adults must practice a *respectful engagement* with the child.

Moral education must be a cooperative enterprise between adult and child. The child needs adult guidance, but in order for the guidance to register, the child must be productively engaged; and in order for such engagement to occur, the child's own initiatives and reactions must be respected. Hence the phrase "respectful engagement." The approach stands in contrast to the laissez-faire romanticism that assumes that children are at their best when left alone. It also stands in contrast to the permissive protectionism that assumes that children cannot cope with straightforward feedback about their moral successes and failures. And it stands in contrast to the indoctrinational approach that assumes that children can learn moral values by passively listening to and blindly following the dictates of authority figures.

The strategies of moral education that I advocate below are drawn from the principles of moral development summarized above. Some of the measures already have been tried out in school programs like those to be discussed in Chapter 8. Such programs represent, I believe, the best of the techniques that moral educators have designed to date. Some of the other measures below have been used less formally by parents and teachers for generations; but they have never been adapted for systematic application in a broad range of educational settings—nor have they been sufficiently documented, evaluated, or disseminated. Still others are new and as yet wholly untried, but they too are based on sound theory and research.

Together, these strategies constitute a comprehensive approach. As such their effectiveness will be greatest when they are employed as part of a total package rather than isolated from one another. Moral education efforts in and out of school have a cumulative effect not so much because the child benefits from hearing the same thing more than once but because morality is largely a matter of adapting fundamental values to a variety of social contexts. As children experience moral thoughts and feelings in diverse social settings, their moral awareness expands correspondingly. Moreover, children's natural moral reactions are strengthened through the pluralistic social support that becomes available through many different types of peer and adult-child relations. An empathic response might receive applause from a peer and silence from a parent, or vice versa; and likewise any act of moral responsibility. Such are the building blocks of a child's moral character.

Although children have natural emotional reactions to moral experiences, there is much that children must learn about how to manage these reactions. First, children must learn to direct their moral emotions towards effective social action. Second, they must learn to modulate their emotional reactions. Raw, primitive emotion—however morally sensitive—is a reliable guide for neither judgment nor conduct.

Above all, children must learn to channel their emotional responses into streams of moral motivation that impel productive action. This requires the ability both to feel the response and to temper it when necessary. The response cannot be lost, but it must be placed in the perspective of realistic knowledge about the limits of social action.

There are dangers of all kinds in failing to learn how to productively modulate one's moral emotions. At the one extreme, one may subdue—or not nurture—one's moral emotions to the extent that they are no longer recognizable. The result is an overall moral insensitivity, leading to a muted sense of shame and guilt and a diminished sense of empathy. At the other extreme, one may allow one's moral emotions to run out of control. Such excess moral emotionalism can take many aberrant forms. One is a debilitating guilt that can never be satiated. A common example of this is the "existential" or "survivor's" guilt that many successful people feel. Psychotherapists' caseloads are full of even more severe examples. Another form of excess moral emotions is directed at others rather than at oneself: an aggressive sense of moral outrage that constantly accompanies one's interpersonal transactions and observations. Both the guilt-ridden and the judgmental manifestations of moral excess impair one's abilities to act in effective and constructive ways towards others.

There is no question that children can learn strategies for modulating their moral emotions at an early age. Moreover, such learning is best done early, since this can help the child avoid establishing maladaptive personality patterns. Robert Hogan and his colleagues have identified three such patterns that can emerge by early adolescence if not prevented.[1] The first is a deeply imbedded pattern of "moral realism": an insensitivity to the needs of others accompanied by a strong awareness of rules. "Moral realists," Hogan writes, "make good bureaucrats and police; but rule following as an end in itself can be detrimental to the welfare of society in those cases where the rules are unjust or dysfunctional."[2] The second maladaptive pattern is "moral enthusiasm": high emotional sensitivity accompanied by a poor social perspective. "Moral enthusiasts are conventionally moral and well-intentioned, but they have no internal moral gyroscope. As a result of their lack of perspective, they rush from one moral cause to another. . . . Their very enthusiasm reduces their effectiveness."[3] The third pattern is "moral zealotry": strong sensitivity with little understanding of social rules or the self's proper role in society. "Zealots are urban guerillas and terrorists who seek aggressive confrontations with authority in the name of social justice."[4] I would add a fourth pattern to this list: a moral self-indulgence that places one's own needs at the center of one's moral concerns. Moral indulgants become outraged at injustices affecting either the self or those with whom they closely identify but remain insensitive to the plights of any others. One example of this in contemporary America is the politician who expresses sympathetic pain for the tax burdens of the wealthy while overlooking the misery of the poor and homeless.

A child's pattern of emotional modulation, whether well or poorly adapted, is directly linked to the manner in which the child has been raised. Maladaptive moral-emotional patterns are prevented in the authoritative type of parenting advocated by Baumrind; for as Baumrind has shown, authoritative child rearing fosters social sensitivity, self-awareness, and respect for rules and authority. The key is the combination of control and reason that authoritative parenting establishes in the child's family life.

One of the many virtues of authoritative parenting is that it poses for the child a fair but firm reality of regulation. This draws the child away from an unguided reliance on internal emotional reactions towards a moral center that is more other-oriented. The child learns to interpret her moral emotions through the examples, advice, and prohibitions provided by mature adults in positions of family authority. This in turn helps the child modulate her moral emotions through actions that fit into the family framework—as, for example, acts of obedience, acts of service, and other contributions to family welfare, order, and harmony.

Authoritative parenting means, among other things, confronting children with the consequences of bad behavior. This means openly expressing one's own emotional responses to the child's misdeeds and clearly explaining the reasons for such reactions. It also means consistently enforcing one's expections for children, both in the positive sense (insisting that children bear their share of personal and family responsibilities) and in a constraining sense (saying no to undesirable behavior).

Many parents in today's culture feel that such demands and restrictions discourage the growth of their child's creative spontaneity. Many parents today refrain from showing their own genuine reactions to their children when the children do not act well; they refuse to enforce expectations for mature behavior and cannot say no to their children consistently and firmly. These are among the most prevalent patterns of belief and behavior in contemporary American families. But in all the psychological literature on creativity and its development, I know of absolutely no scientific evidence in support of this view. There are, on the other hand, several good, empirically confirmed reasons to believe that *not* enforcing such expectations and restrictions places children in severe characterological risk.

The problem with not enforcing such expectations and restrictions is that it allows children to place their own emotional reactions at the center of their moral concerns. The children will learn only to listen to their own inner responses, becoming their own moral self-referents. As a consequence, they will not learn habits of respect for adults or other authority figures beyond themselves. They may find out at a later time that they cannot get their way without giving verbal or behavioral lip service to the demands of people more powerful than they. But this will just teach them manipulation, disingenuity, and, ultimately, prevarication with themselves as well as others.

If children are allowed to become their own moral self-referents, they will come to deny wrongdoing no matter how poorly they act. In their eyes, they have done nothing wrong. Because they have not developed sufficient respect for others, they do not care deeply about what others think (as long as they have done the minimum necessary to get their way). So the opinions of others, as well as the external evidence, become secondary to the child's own inner feelings; and the child tells himself whatever he needs to hear in order to bolster these feelings. This emotional self-indulgence—fostered by the overindulgant parent—leads to a repeated pattern of self-deception as well as indifference to truthful discourse with others. It also breeds an arrogant disregard for others' opinions and an exaggerated feeling of self-worth.

In contrast, children who are presented with clear, consistent expectations learn to orient their feelings outwards as well as inwards. They learn to accommodate to regulation and constraint in a cooperative rather than manipulative way. Their voluntary submission arises out of genuine understanding and agreement rather than for the sake of show. In the process, they become attuned to their most other-oriented moral emotions: empathy, shame (concern for the respect of others), and guilt (concerns for moral principles that transcend one's selfish desires). The child's respect for others, encouraged through authoritative parenting, nurtures the child's moral emotions. Open communication between authoritative parent and child in turn helps the child modulate these feelings in a productive way.

Authoritative parenting is a general pattern of action and belief that is consistent with the overarching principle of respectful engagement that I have introduced. Also consistent with this principle are a number of more specific and limited measures. These measures all serve the same purpose, without requiring holistic alterations in every parent-child relation. All follow the general principle of "respectful engagement" in the sense that they respond to the child's own experience without intruding upon this experience, while at the same time presenting the child with consistent expectations, guidelines, and mature insights clearly explained.

My first specific recommendation is that parents should share openly with children moral reactions to events in their own adult lives. Sharing emotional reactions means demonstrating them when appropriate, describing them clearly, and answering children's questions about them candidly. The purpose here is to allow children to observe how respected adults manage moral feelings, thus providing children with models of emotional modulation.

This may sound deceptively simple, yet in American life today it is probably the least followed of all the measures that I propose. In my observations, the current operating mode is to shelter children from the realities of adult emotional response. This is done in a number of ways and for a number of reasons. The parent may not wish to expose the child to demonstrations of the parent's guilt, anger, fear, or uncertainty. Such exposure, however, is exactly what children need in order to learn ways of dealing with their own moral emotions. Let us take one example as a case in point. This particular example is invented, but it does represent a variation on some real instances that I have observed in my personal and professional life.

Dr. Smith is a dentist who runs his practice out of an office suite in his home. He takes what he thinks of as an "aggressive" approach to his income taxes, attributing a very large proportion of his gardening, repair, utilities, and other household bills to the dental business. One winter he attends a professional conference in the Caribbean and brings his family. Again, he takes an aggressive approach and writes off the whole trip, including most of his family's expenses. When his name happens to come up for an IRS audit, many of Dr. Smith's deductions are ruled inappropriate. He is forced to pay sizable back taxes and is also assessed a penalty for misrepresenting his expenses. The tax bill and penalty are heavy enough to sharply curtail the family's spending plans for the next couple of years. Because of this, the children become aware that there has been some sort of problem in the family, and on several occasions ask for an explanation.

Now Dr. Smith is embarrassed about his delinquent behavior and does not want to have his children think that their father is a dishonest man. He is afraid that this will set a poor example for them, and of course he would rather avoid the further embarrassment of bringing the situation to light. He also harbors some feeling that he was wronged—not so much by the IRS judgment, which he admits to himself was technically correct, but by their decision to go after *him* when there are so many "fat cats" out there who abuse the system so much more. In short, Dr. Smith's feelings are a confusing mixture of embarrassment, self-pity, and mild outrage. He can think of no clear message to give his children about the episode, and he feels that it is important to "save face" with them. He therefore discourages family discussion of the incident, maintaining simply that "some mistakes were made" in his business transactions, that it is a private matter, and that it will be straightened out eventually.

Dr. Smith has adopted a course of action that is probably normal in our society, and I certainly sympathize with his reasons for it. But I believe that it is a mistaken course of action. It requires him to practice deception with his children, even if this is only a deception by omission. Children have ways of eventually discovering the truth about family matters, and the awareness that their father has deceived them will set a worse example for them than anything that he could have told them about his IRS troubles. Dr. Smith's course of action has also deprived him of a valuable opportunity to morally educate his children.

There are many lessons that Dr. Smith's children could have learned from this episode if he had chosen to open his feelings to them. First, they would have seen that even decent, competent, and respected adults sometimes experience moral problems that are difficult to handle emotionally. They would have seen that moral issues like honesty and cheating are often ambiguous and subject to interpretation—and that one's own interpretation often must succumb to the rulings of persons in authority. They would have seen their father wrestling to accept the decision of the authorities in this case, and perhaps would have seen him learn something from the incident. Ultimately, they would have seen him sort out and modulate his own emotional responses to this difficult situation. Adults can give children no better learning opportunity than this kind of firsthand look at mature adaptation to a formidable challenge.

The other educational benefit of open expression is the message that honesty is a primary virtue. It is not tenable to profess the value of truth if it is not practiced consistently in the family. Too often adults believe that the truth must be shaded to protect their children from damaging observations and feelings. However, as in the above example, the observations and feelings that are hidden from children are often those that could provide the most productive moral lessons. Moreover, when children become aware that the truth has been shaded—as they eventually do—they receive precisely the wrong kind of moral message. Frank communication about problems and emotions may seem risky, difficult, and embarrassing for a parent, but it is one of the most effective educational gifts that an adult can bestow upon a child.

Children should be encouraged to recognize their own moral feelings and urged to discuss them with the adults in their lives. The purposes here are (1) to support and nurture children's moral reactions, (2) to help children identify these moral reactions, (3) to encourage children's expressions of their moral reactions in thought and deed, and (4) to help children gain control of their moral emotions so that their expressions of these emotions serve the social good.

At the present time, it is striking how few efforts are made to encourage children's awareness of their moral emotions. I know of no formal moral education program that directs its efforts towards children's moral emotions. Nor do parents typically do so in their discussions with children about moral issues. In general, parents and other adults are more accustomed to giving children directives than to asking children about their own feelings.

Adult indifference to children's moral feelings may be understandable, for adults do have far more knowledge of most moral issues than do children. But only children can monitor their own inner moral reactions. This is one reason why it is so important that children learn to recognize and interpret their feelings for themselves. Another reason is that regulating one's private emotional life is a difficult task for anyone, child or adult. Early learning can play a critical role in mastering this task, preventing the serious risk of later failure.

We know that normal childhood emotional confusions about moral issues can turn into enduring psychological conflict if allowed to persist. One example of this can be found in the development of certain forms of severe neurotic guilt. It is normal and benign for children to confuse their guilt over a misdeed with their fear of punishment for the misdeed. This childhood confusion is aided and abetted by the cognitive confusion called "immanent justice" described in Chapter 5. The child believes that moral infractions inevitably lead to unhappy consequences of a physical sort: if the boy tells a lie, he will be hit by a falling tree branch, for example. Children outgrow this cognitive confusion when they have enough experience to realize that people sometimes do—at least in the physical sense—"get away" with bad acts. But the associated emotional confusion can linger, to the detriment of one's later sense of well-being. It is common for people long after childhood to experience a dread that they cannot place after committing an act that they sense is wrong. This is why guilt and fear are often confused in the mental experience of troubled adolescents and adults. In extreme cases where there is also a tendency to exaggerate the significance of one's actions, this kind of guilt-induced dread can become a generalized and crippling anxiety.

Early experience in introspection and self-monitoring can help children identify guilt and other moral emotions that they naturally experience. Adults can help children identify their emotions by discussing the children's feelings, introducing distinctions that the child may not yet know, and offering related examples from the adults' own lives. This in turn would help children separate these moral feelings from their fears about real physical dangers. It is just this kind of treatment that takes place in psychotherapy when patients complain of unmanageable fears and painful emotional confusions. But sound early educational encounters can prevent these kinds of confusions from being carried over to adulthood, where they can pose a continuing threat to one's affective stability. Children can learn to become attuned to their own inner life. As a result, they can learn to channel their moral emotions into constructive social action rather than turning them into exaggerated and debilitating fears.

Because morality is fundamentally concerned with one's obligations to others, it cannot be developed solely through introspection and recognition of one's inner feelings, however morally oriented these feelings may be. Training children in emotional self-monitoring can enable them to control and productively channel their moral emotions, but in itself it is an incomplete educational measure. Children must learn to become attuned not only to their own emotional reactions but also to those of others. This provides a means of correcting the imbalances and distortions that inevitably arise in one's personal reactions to events. To prevent such imbalances, children must learn to be receptive to the input from others' emotional expressions, modifying their own feelings when appropriate. Yet they must also learn to recognize when their own reactions provide the truest moral indicator on a given occasion, becoming able at times to resist the distractions and "noise" of other peoples' emotional expressions.

Children should be exposed to conceptual frameworks that juxtapose their own moral reactions against those of others. This exposure will enable them to realize that others have interests and beliefs that often will clash with their own. It also will enable them to orient toward both their own feelings and those of others, and to understand the relations between the two. All of this helps children establish the conceptual and interpersonal balance necessary for a mature understanding and appreciation of justice.

Creating this kind of balance is no easy challenge. Undoubtedly it is a lifelong task; but, like all essential developmental achievements, it is best begun early. The central elements that are needed here are (1) an awareness of the others' feelings, (2) an awareness of one's own feelings, (3) a sense of how the two are related—that is, how they compare and contrast, and how they may influence one another, and (4) an internal "moral compass" that enables the child to make critical choices about when to veer towards the self's reactions and when to veer towards those of the other.

The first three of these elements can be addressed by training children's social perspective-taking skills. The fourth element, an internal "moral compass," can be established only by a mature sense of justice. Perspective taking and a mature sense of justice both require strong intellectual as well as affective awareness. Both entail cognitive activities in which the developmental course of a child's moral understanding and that of the child's moral emotions deeply interpenetrate. Educational programs in the schools, as we shall see in Chapter 8, can do much to enhance children's moral understanding. Parents should support such programs and amplify their effectiveness through informed discussions on the home front.

There is no more effective facilitator of moral development than fostering children's willingness to take responsibility for good and bad deeds. Taking responsibility for good deeds means responding to another's needs with effective prosocial action. Taking responsibility for bad deeds means admitting culpability when one has acted wrongly, accepting just punishment, and making restitution for the wrong that one has done when this is possible. This sense of responsibility goes to the heart of moral character—what once was commonly called "moral fiber." Neither the most empathic emotional response, the sharpest awareness, nor the best of intentions can do very much for the social good if one lacks the strength of character necessary to take responsibility for one's actions.

Parents certainly have a role in building their children's moral character. Authoritative child-rearing patterns contribute significantly to children's senses of social and personal responsibility. But holistic child-rearing patterns are deeply entrenched and not readily altered. Is there anything else that can be done in the home or school to build character and foster children's willingness to assume moral responsibility?

There are no shortcuts to moral character. Positive steps in this direction may require difficult—and even severe—adjustments in our treatment of children and in our expectations for them. The only satisfactory means of training responsibility in our young is to offer them serious opportunities to assume such responsibility, sharing with them the full expectation that they indeed will do so.

Once again the principle of respectful engagement comes into play. Encouraging children to assume responsibility means in part giving them responsibility, which in turn implies trusting them to rise to the occasion. Children are therefore respected as potentially responsible persons. But such respect is also accompanied by a certain social pressure. There must be an expectation, and at times an insistence, that children accept rather than ignore their moral responsibilities. This requires respectful engagement.

None of this comes easily, particularly for those of us living in contemporary Western society. One of the fruits of technology and affluence has been the reduced need to rely on children for real help around the house or at work. In many agrarian societies, children are assigned serious chores: caring for younger siblings, assisting in the family trade, and so on. Anthropologists have noted that such service has a positive effect on these children's sense of social responsibility.[5] Even in our own society, it was not so long ago that children commonly were seen as serving an essential economic need for their families.[6] With progress, we became able to relieve our children of such service, offering them instead an extended period of life devoted to their own education and self-development. But we have paid a price in eliminating many of the experiences from which children derived their willingness to assume responsibility.

I believe that we need to return to some of our earlier expectations for children's service—if not now for economic reasons, for their own moral welfare. Children and adolescents certainly should have ample time for exploration, play, and education. But childhood and adolescence should not be devoted to self-indulgence or even to the sole pursuit of personal skills and talents. For the optimal development of moral character, a child needs to experience the responsibilities and rewards of genuine service while still young.

Only through real service can children learn what it means to have others rely on them, to be entrusted with an important function, and to bear the credit or blame for a necessary job well or poorly done. Obviously I do not advocate a return to child labor: my suggestion is for judicious work assignments only, with the child's social and intellectual development as the overriding goals. Such assignments need to be tailored to the child's abilities. But the nature of our expectations must change. Rather than believing that children must be shielded from real obligations for as long as possible, we need to do precisely the opposite: entrust them with serious functions as soon as they are ready and able to perform them. In this way moral responsibility can become habitual from an early age, and the way paved for the development of sturdy moral character.

8

·

Teaching Values
in the Schools

At first glance, the notion of teaching children moral values in public schools might seem controversial in a nonsectarian, pluralistic society like our own. After all, shouldn't schools in a democracy concentrate on the "three r's" and leave questions of morality to pupils' families and churches? Indeed, this has become America's solution to the problem of religious instruction. As a means of avoiding the unsolvable problem of which religious beliefs to cover, we have chosen to exclude religion entirely from the classroom. This has proven to be a controversial solution, but the controversies do not challenge the basic premise of religious neutrality. For example, even those who advocate inserting time for prayer back into the public school day would keep the prayer time "silent"—that is, doctrinally empty.

Unlike religious instruction, however, morality cannot be excluded from the classroom, no matter how hard one tries. It is part of the very fabric of schooling. In their efforts to create an atmosphere conducive to learning, teachers constantly draw their pupils' attention to the standards of orderliness, respect for others, the work ethic, honesty, and responsibility. Working hard, keeping quiet, being punctual, acting polite to the teacher, being neat, helping classmates without cheating, refraining from stealing or fighting, are all standards that teachers commonly demand. In the process, basic moral values are communicated to the young. These values, implicit in every procedure and demand of the school setting, are taken from the culture that has produced the school and remain generally consistent with those of the culture. The school provides an important training ground for learning and mastering these values.

Even requiring a child to attend regularly, for the greater part of her waking life, an institution devoted to ideas and intellectual skills makes a statement to the young about what is valued by society at large. (In fact, some communal subcultures traditionally have objected to compulsory education on exactly these grounds.) Academic achievement and "book learning" themselves are values, and as such are matters of human choice. By their very existence, schools endorse these values. This is one of many reasons why schools have always been, and will always be, in the business of moral education.

Nevertheless, there remain unresolved questions about whether schools should spend time *directly* teaching moral values; and, if so, which moral values. These questions recently have acquired increased urgency because of contemporary social conditions. Observers frequently worry that we are witnessing a moral degeneration of youth in our society. Drug abuse, delinquency, and teenage pregnancy abound; genuine commitment to ideals seems rare. In response, educators have developed programs explicitly dedicated to moral growth.

Many schools have adopted such programs, and many have declined to do so. Perhaps all educators have wondered whether such programs can alleviate the social problems that are so prevalent in schools and in society today. Some believe that special moral education programs have the potential to address such problems, whereas others believe that such programs at best waste time and at worst foster the wrong values and give children the wrong message about their true obligations.

What has been missing in this debate is an informed use of available scientific knowledge. From research and observations in the schools, we have at our disposal direct evidence on the effects of various moral education programs. Further, the studies described throughout this book offer us a solid base of knowledge about children's morality and the conditions that best foster it. The conclusions that we can readily draw from all of this research offer us answers to our pressing contemporary questions about moral education and its optimal uses.

Two approaches focusing on children's moral reasoning spread widely throughout North American schools in the 1970s and 80s. The two approaches have much in common, especially their use of provocative questions and classroom discussion and training techniques. Both aim to make children more thoughtful about the importance of values in social life. But the two approaches are divided by deep theoretical schisms that make a dramatic difference in the moral perspectives that they communicate to children. The first of these approaches has been called the "values clarifying approach," or *values clarification*. The second is the *cognitive-developmental* approach to moral education.

Values clarification was introduced by Louis Raths, Merrill Harmin, and Sidney Simon in an influential 1966 book, *Values and Teaching*.[1] The book reflects many popular sentiments of its time. Children should be free to choose their own values; "moralizing" and "indoctrination" are hazardous to intellectual growth; schools should take pains to foster self-esteem and personal liberty rather than particular attitudes or beliefs. The approach is assertively "values neutral." In the terms of our Chapter 6 discussion of moral philosophy, it is relativistic in the extreme.

The three cherished goals of values clarification are choosing, prizing, and acting. Children are to be encouraged (1) to choose their values freely from among as many alternatives as possible, (2) to prize and affirm their choices, whatever they may be, and (3) to act upon their values consistently throughout their daily life.

The approach does not presume to identify or justify these values for the child. In fact, the opposite is advocated. Teachers should avoid overly directive questions or remarks that might suggest the superiority of some values over others. The point is to clarify the possibilities so that children can make their own well-informed choices. Then the tasks become helping children feel secure in these choices and helping make their values public through word and deed.

In order to accomplish this, teachers are given a number of strategies for classroom use. The most general of these is "the clarifying response." Whenever a student says or does something that implies a value, teachers are advised to ask a noncommittal question that encourages the child to discuss the value more fully. The student could be asked about what the value means, about whether he has thought about any alternatives, about how he came to adopt the value, or about how he feels about the value.

The teacher is given two cautions. First, the clarifying response must avoid "moralizing, criticizing, giving values, or evaluating. The adult excludes all hints of 'good' or 'right' or 'acceptable.'"[2] Second, the exchange engendered by the response must be brief. The student must not feel pressured to come up with moral platitudes for the occasion: "The idea, without moralizing, is to raise a few questions, leave them hanging in the air, and then move on."[3] For this reason, teachers' clarifying responses and the ensuing brief discussions are considered "one-legged conferences." Two examples follow:

Example 1

STUDENT: I believe that all men are created equal.

TEACHER: What do you mean by that?

STUDENT: I guess that I mean that all people are equally good and none should have advantages over others.

TEACHER: Does this idea suggest that some changes need to be made in our world, even in this school and this town?

STUDENT: Oh, lots of them. Want me to name some?

TEACHER: No, we have to get back to our spelling lesson, but I was just wondering if you were working on any of those changes, actually trying to bring them about.

STUDENT: Not yet, but I may soon.

TEACHER: I see. Now, back to the spelling list. . . .[4]

Example 2

TEACHER: You say, Glenn, that you are a liberal in political matters?

GLENN: Yes, I am.

TEACHER: Where did your ideas come from?

GLENN: Well, my parents I guess, mostly.

TEACHER: Are you familiar with other positions?

GLENN: Well, sort of.

TEACHER: I see, Glenn. Now, class, getting back to the homework for today. . . .[5]

Sometimes teachers themselves introduce values during planned "values discussions." Again the teacher is warned against leading the child towards preordained notions of right and wrong. This, of course, can be a difficult challenge for teachers when the discussion turns to issues close to home. In the following discussion, the teacher struggles to maintain her role as an enforcer of classroom order while still refraining from taking a position on the general value of honesty:

TEACHER: So some of you think it is best to be honest on tests, is that right? (Some heads nod affirmatively.) And some of you think dishonesty is all right? (A few hesitant and slight nods.) And I guess some of you are not certain. (Heads nod.) Well, are there any choices, or is it just a matter of honesty or dishonesty?

SAM: You could be honest some of the time and dishonest some of the time.

TEACHER: Does that sound like a possible choice, class? (Heads nod.) Any other alternatives to choose from?

TRACY: You could be honest in some situations and not in others. For example, I am not honest when a friend asks me about an ugly dress, at least sometimes. (Laughter.)

TEACHER: Is that a possible choice, class? (Heads nod again.) Any other alternatives?

SAM: It seems to me that you have to be all one way or the other.

TEACHER: Just a minute, Sam. As usual we are first looking for the alternatives that there are in the issue. Later . . . you can discuss this and see if you are able to make a choice and if you want to make your choice part of your actual behavior. That is something you must do for yourself.

GINGER: Does this mean that we can decide for ourselves whether we should be honest on tests here?

TEACHER: No, that means that you can decide on the value. I personally value honesty; and although you may choose to be dishonest, I shall insist that we be honest on our tests here. In other areas of your life, you may have more freedom to be dishonest, but one can't do anything any time, and in this class I shall expect honesty on tests.

GINGER: But how can we decide for ourselves? Aren't you telling us what to value?

TEACHER: Not exactly. I don't mean to tell you what you should value. That's up to you. But I do mean that in this class, not elsewhere necessarily, you have to be honest on tests or suffer consequences. I merely mean that I cannot give tests without the rule of honesty. All of you who choose dishonesty as a value may not practice it here, that's all I'm saying. Further questions anyone?[6]

In addition to conducting these types of public discussions, teachers also can give students written stories and questions called "value sheets." The story might tell of people evading payment at a toll booth, two friends teasing an outsider, or someone failing to respond to a stranger's screams. The children are asked to write down their own views on these matters. In this way each child is given a chance to express values apart from the glare of the group. In later individual feedback sessions, the teacher can help each child further understand the value implications of the child's written statements.

Still other exercises include student diaries, interviews with parents and other adults outside the classroom, reports, and classroom forums. All of these techniques help students appreciate the range of alternative values in the world and help them position themselves freely amongst these values. Ideally students come away with a realization of how important values are in everyday life, a sense of what their own values are, a willingness to reexamine their values in light of other possibilities, and a commitment to act according to their final value choices.

Values clarification has made inroads into American public education because it avoids controversies about which values should be espoused in a community school. As far as is ever possible, it espouses none beyond the implicit statement that values themselves are important.

But the approach's value neutrality poses problems of its own. Teachers, like other adults, act as models for children. If a teacher publicly withholds judgment about moral issues, what kind of message is communicated to the student? Are students in fact being trained to tolerate all values, whether right or wrong, good or evil? How can a teacher *not* take a position on honesty? Are there not, indeed, some values that are so central to our society, and to humanity in general, that positions of neutrality relative to them become morally unacceptable?

These are some of the questions that arise as we read the teacher-student clarification dialogues quoted above. It seems odd, for example, to curtail a values conversation just as a child is about to volunteer information about how he would change the world (Example 1). Clearly this was intended to indicate that the child must work out such matters for himself. But are such ruminations best thought of as private, individual choices? Shouldn't the adult take the opportunity here to offer the child more directed guidance? One certainly can understand why a teacher would avoid commenting on the soundness of political liberalism (Example 2). But when the issue switches to a commonly accepted virtue like honesty (Example 3), abstaining from expressing one's moral beliefs seems itself a moral choice—and a rather irresponsible one at that, given the importance of adult guidance for introducing children to basic premises of the moral order (see Chapter 4).

Unlike values clarification, the cognitive-developmental approach assumes that some moral positions are indeed better than others. In the course of development, children naturally tend to acquire more advanced modes of thought. These advanced modes are ethically superior to those that preceded them developmentally, because they solve a wider range of social problems, they are less self-oriented, and they more strongly reflect universal values such as fairness and human rights.[7] As we have seen, as children develop they reorganize their ideas about empathy, justice, authority, and friendship. These changes can be represented as progressive sequences of moral and social conceptions. The operating assumption behind such sequences is that the higher levels are more cogent than the lower ones, i.e., that development means improvement.

From the cognitive-developmental perspective, the job of the teacher is "promoting moral growth" rather than simply encouraging children to come to terms with their own freely chosen values. Moral growth implies a predefined directionality towards the values represented by the higher moral judgment levels. Honesty and dishonesty, for example, are not seen as two alternatives with equivalent moral status. Honesty is the better value because it shows respect for the rights of others to know the truth. Acquiring more sophisticated modes of moral judgment means learning how fundamental values like honesty can be implemented and coordinated with other essential values in increasingly complex life situations. It does *not* mean learning to equivocate about the moral correctness of such values.

The cognitive-developmental approach encourages teachers not only to engage children in moral discussion, but also to use such discussion as an opportunity to foster higher forms of moral judgment. This is done by exposing students to higher reasoning forms in techniques such as "plus one matching." During debates about values, the teacher gauges the typical developmental level of a student's judgments. The teacher then introduces an alternative perspective derived from a moral judgment position that is just one level higher than the student's level. The teachers comments are "matched" to the student's judgmental level, but a bit more advanced. This technique was drawn from experimental research showing that "plus one" exposure is the most effective means of inducing positive moral change.[8]

Ideally the matching technique creates both an incentive for children to reexamine their own values and a suggestion that there is a better mode of moral judgment available to them. An example might be a teacher's response when a child says that revenge is the best policy if someone hurts you. The teacher knows that retribution can be an enormously complex issue. It is tied to the conflicting aims of gaining "sweet" retribution, carrying out punitive justice, and creating a preventive disincentive for further wrongdoing. It also must be modified by the requirements of charity and mercy and by the knowledge that revenge can maintain a never-ending cycle of hostile acts. The teacher might feel that the child's statements reflect little appreciation of such issues. For example, the child might not yet understand the charitable message of the Golden Rule (see Chapter 5), which the teacher might believe to be a better value than eye-for-eye revenge. The teacher's job, therefore is to foster in the child a perspectives on retribution that incorporates the moral message of the Golden Rule and joins this message with the child's other real-world concerns.

This effort might be initiated by saying, "If I were the boy that you hit back, that would give me another reason to act mean to you, so then you would be back where you started from." It could be followed with probing questions: "How would you feel if you were the other kid?" "Which is more important, to hurt someone who has done something wrong or to stop them from doing it?" "If you were the one who started the fight, what would be the best way for the other guy to handle it?"

Such directed statements and questions may lead a child to a sense of the true rationale behind the Golden Rule. This could be a significant advance for a child who previously was acquainted only with tit-for-tat rules of exchange. This instruction, however, will not produce for the child a comprehensive, working theory of retributive justice in society. This would be well beyond the child's capabilities. For this reason, the cognitive-developmental approach advocates matching the instructional goals to the child's developmental level.

In practice, it is neither easy nor always possible for teachers to assess children's judgmental capacities in the course of classroom conversations. Teachers are too busy, and things in the classroom happen too quickly, for this kind of running assessment. In fact, even if classroom events could be momentarily frozen for just this purpose, the reliability of teachers' on-the-spot readings of students' moral judgment levels would be shaky at best. Consequently, "plus one matching" remains something of an ideal, and is necessarily bolstered in the cognitive-developmental approach by several other pedagogical techniques.

The most common of these are peer classroom discussions of moral dilemmas introduced by the teacher. Students debate with one another about the best resolution of a conflict involving justice and human rights. The teacher's role is to initiate the discussion and to draw out students' reasons for their statements. In the course of such discussions, many conflicting points of view will be expressed. As students consider such conflicts, they reexamine their own perspectives and begin molding new ones. The teacher facilitates this process by encouraging students to explicate their opinions in depth, thus sharpening any conflicts that might exist between members of the group. But, unlike the values clarification approach, the teacher makes public his own moral reactions to the question under debate.

Supplementing these discussion methods are indirect counseling techniques that are known to trigger developmental processes. For example, since role taking has been shown to be at the heart of moral judgment, children are given exercises that place them in the roles of real and imaginary others. Similarly, there are exercises that train children's capacities for empathy, their listening skills, and their communication skills, all of which have been shown to be important in the formation of advanced moral judgment. In addition, children are guided towards popular readings that demonstrate moral values at or just above their developmental levels.

Many of these techniques do bear some similarity to those used in values clarification. Classroom discussion of moral problems, role taking and empathy training, and the practice of listening skills all play a part in both approaches. The difference lies in the ultimate message that teachers communicate throughout these and other exercises. For values clarification, the goals are awareness, toleration, and individual choice. In the cognitive-developmental approach, the goal is acquiring more advanced forms of moral judgment. This is why teachers practicing the latter approach are more directive in shaping classroom discussions. They ask suggestive questions, point out contradictions, and directly assert basic values when they consider it important to do so.

There have been a number of studies assessing the effects and effectiveness of the two approaches. Educational psychologist Alan Lockwood reviewed these studies and looked at all the benefits claimed by proponents of both approaches.[9] These included, from the values clarification approach, improved self-esteem, personal adjustment, reading ability, values awareness, attitudes about science and ecology, classroom behavior, and reduced drug usage. For the cognitive-developmental approach, the main claimed benefit was maturity of moral judgment. From the extensive evidence available, it is clear that the values clarification approach does not live up to its ambitious claims. The cognitive-developmental approach, in contrast, does live up to its claims; but its claims may not be ambitious enough.

There is, for example, little evidence that values clarification improves children's self-esteem or personal adjustment. Effects on reading ability and attitudes about science are so small as to be questionable. Most problematic is the program's lack of impact on values, the heart of the effort. As Lockwood writes, "Based on these studies, there is no evidence that values clarification has a systematic, demonstrated impact on students' values."[10] The one redeeming finding is that, according to teachers' perceptions, children's classroom behavior does improve somewhat during values clarification discussions. This improved behavior, however, does not generalize to the rest of the school day; nor does it result in other benefits, such as decreased drug abuse.

There is, on the other hand, considerable evidence that the cognitive-developmental approach does stimulate children's moral judgment. Most effective within this approach are the direct discussion techniques. Systematic programs of moral discussion, led by a teacher familiar with developmental theory and objectives, consistently result in significant advances in children's moral reasoning skills. Still effective, but less consistently so, are indirect techniques such as role taking, empathy, and communications training. For both direct and indirect techniques, the younger the child, the greater the benefit.

The major remaining question is whether the judgmental advances fostered by cognitive-developmental training make a difference in the real world of moral (and immoral) action. Practitioners of this approach have not carefully examined this critical question: "Researchers would provide an important service by identifying the extent to which changes in moral reasoning are associated with observable or inferred changes in the behavioral, affective, and cognitive realms."[11] Until they do, we shall have little evidence either way concerning the ultimate value of teaching moral reasoning; and without such information, public schools may well decide that there are insufficient grounds for adopting moral education programs that focus chiefly on reasoning.

Not all contemporary approaches to moral education limit themselves to judgment and reasoning, however. At the present time, schools throughout American are experimenting with attempts to build "moral character," to encourage moral conduct, and even to improve the "moral atmosphere" of the classroom. These approaches are to some extent in competition with one another, since they are founded upon conflicting beliefs about the proper aims of moral education. Although the tradition from which they have sprung dates back to the earliest days of public education, the recent attempts are very new, and have not been adequately evaluated through carefully designed research.

Educator Edward Wynne believes that moral reasoning programs cannot fulfill the promise of character education.[12] In the "great tradition" of early American schooling, Wynne writes, schools unambiguously espoused virtues like promptness, neatness, respect for authority, and truth-telling. Compliance was rewarded and violations were punished. Emphasis was on the acquisition of good behavioral habits rather than on the development of complex reasoning skills. This was the period between 1880 and 1930, before the dramatic postwar rise in youth delinquency, suicide, drug abuse, and pregnancy.

Was there a connection between this traditional form of moral education and the seemingly more socialized conduct of youth in those days? Wynne believes so, although the data are not exactly on his side. The large-scale Hartshorne and May study, discussed earlier, specifically examined the behavior of students who had been exposed to formal character education training. Hartshorne and May found little relation between exposure to such programs and good (e.g., honest, responsible) conduct in students. In fact, some have attributed the decline of traditional character education in public schools to the influence of Hartshorne and May's widely disseminated report.

But Wynne and others believe that the educational establishment abandoned such efforts too quickly. "Ironically, the research findings of Hartshorne and May did not conflict with . . . the great tradition. The tradition emphasized that moral formation was complex. To be effective, it had to be incremental, diverse, pervasive, persistent, and rigorous."[13] Short-term experimentation might well miss these effects. Over a period of many years, frequent and consistent instruction may indeed create good values and good habits in students.

Wynne calls for a return to "character education" approaches that focus on children's conduct and that are forthright in their espousal of traditional moral values. He believes that "indoctrination" should cease being a dirty word in the educational community. Although he does not dismiss the importance of moral judgment, he considers it secondary to everyday, often mundane, standards of conduct. In Wynne's stance one is reminded of Spinoza's old aphorism, "The palace of reasoning may be entered only through the courtyard of habit."

Wynne's own character education efforts focus more on the school setting than on the individual child. With a group of educators in the Chicago area, Wynne has devised a school recognition program called "For Character." Schools are assessed, initially by themselves and later by a team of site visitors, in terms of how well they contribute to the formation of students' moral character. Character is defined "in a rather traditional fashion: not hurting others—observing discipline; and going out of one's way to be polite, truthful, and helpful to others."[14]

Awards are given annually to top-ranking schools. Criteria for excellence include both social and academic expectations maintained by the school. Schools are thereby induced to ask themselves the following questions: Do we have a conduct code, and is it rigorously and consistently enforced? How much homework is expected? Is homework regularly completed by a good proportion of students? Do we have rewards for effort and recognition of meritorious performance?

Special attention is paid to extracurricular associations that a school may sponsor. Are there service clubs, team sports, student-to-student tutoring programs? Do such activities provide students with occasions for helping and a sense of group loyalty? Wynne emphasizes the character-building role of school teams and clubs in the days of "the great tradition": "These groups were important reference points for communicating values, among them, group loyalty, and the diverse incidents of group life provided occasions for object lessons."[15] He sees no reason why such groups could not play the same character-building role in the America of today.

The function of Wynne's recognition awards is to publicly highlight the qualities that Wynne and his colleagues believe will bring back to American schools the serious enterprise of character education. Clearly some of these qualities recall a bygone era. Wynne writes of some unifying features that he has noticed in excellent schools with "good spirit." These include dress codes for both teachers and students; frequent use of mottos, school symbols, songs, and colors; ceremonies, parades, pep rallies, flag salutes; student-faculty games, "well-organized" parties, "days for wearing silly costumes," and so on. In many schools in America today, of course, such events would seem as foreign as a spring tulip festival, but Wynne believes that they can be brought back with credibility.

There is more to this approach than pure nostalgia. Wynne has isolated precisely those features of school life that engage children in activities that require cooperation with the collective and a turning away from self-absorption. This is a different moral priority than the individualistic free choice promoted by values clarification. But it may be one that is as much in tune with the times today as it was when the "great tradition" was founded.

Former Secretary of Education William Bennett also endorses character education and is critical of reasoning-centered approaches such as values clarification and cognitive moral development.[16] He argues, first, that these approaches emphasize reflection and neglect habit. Second, they remove morality from the real, natural contexts in which moral choices must be made. Third, they present morality as an exercise in problem solving and decision making rather than as the day-to-day good behavior that it really is. He writes:

Because values educationists view moral life principally as a matter of making decisions about dilemmas in morally problematic matters, the ethically significant collapses into the ethically problematic. The problematic approach denies the most important part of morality, which is not the development of decision-making capacities, but the development of what used to be called, and can still be called, character—that is, dispositions and habits of the mind and heart. A moral educationist's model moral person is one who is always in doubt, in dilemma, tearing his hair out, trying to get clear about what to do. The moral individual, however, is rarely presented as a conscientious person, a person of character and equanimity, who, because of his character, doesn't have to face hard decisions every ten minutes or every ten days.[17]

Bennett believes that moral instruction should permeate the entire school curriculum and school day. To be effective, school teachers and administrators must teach values whenever moral questions arise, whether this be in discussions of current events or in analyses of classic history and literature. "It is misguided to isolate instruction about morality . . . from the contexts in which it naturally arises . . . matters of moral import should be discussed when they arise, as they inevitably will, as real issues."[18] Further, teachers should be unequivocal in their defense of the right values; and they should embody these values in their daily behavior so as to provide good role models for their pupils.

Bennett is right in his assumption that children learn morality best in the natural contexts of real social interaction. If there were any doubts about this, the research discussed throughout this book should put them to rest. But his suggestion that too much moral reasoning and reflection somehow could work against the building of a child's moral character stands without logical or empirical support.

Bennett imagines an opposition between moral reflection on the one hand and moral habit on the other. In light of all available evidence, this opposition does not exist. I know of no study showing that the development of moral reflection is inimical to the acquisition of moral habit. To the contrary, virtually all the relevant studies show that sophistication in moral reasoning goes hand in hand with consistent, reliable moral conduct. Moral judgment and action support one another throughout the course of a child's development. Although advances in one do not invariably lead to improvements in the other, they often do; and there is no evidence whatsoever that they could have any deleterious effect.

In fact, Bennett's aversion to conscious moral decision making is itself so misguided as to present a threat to the very democratic traditions that he professes to cherish. Habit without reflection is adaptive only in a totalitarian climate. It hardly provides a goal for moral education in a democratic society. As one critic of this position, psychologist and educator Elliot Turiel, observes:

> The message from character education proponents seems to be that in this realm the examined life is corrupting. It is a curious state of affairs in which many of the features usually regarded as part of a good education—analysis, intellectual scrutiny, informed self-correction—are considered miseducative.[19]

In the writings of Wynne, Bennett, and many others holding similar views, there seems to be an odd assumption that democratic values can be effectively transmitted to youth without also fostering the capacity to make autonomous moral choices. Conservative politician Jeane Kirkpatrick, for example, has written a statement about moral education in which she suggests that teachers directly indoctrinate their students in democratic ideals.[20]

The irony in all of this is that these ideologically driven writings commit the precise error that they have warned against: they disembody the ideals that they wish transmit from the child's everday social interactions. Democracy, to take just one example, cannot be taught as a moral abstraction. Nor is it effectively conveyed solely through second-hand accounts found in world politics, history, or literature. It is learned, as all values are learned, through the child's active participation in experiences that foster democratic thought and action. One such experience is making freely autonomous moral choices. Another such experience is openly discussing those choices, without fear of reprisal, in public debate with peers. These are precisely the experiences that reasoning-based moral education programs offer.

A child's social experience determines the course of the child's moral development. This experience is important not only because it exposes children to new ideas but also because it engages children in relationships that are conducted through essential rules and procedures. Children learn the rules and procedures that apply to the relationships in which they participate. For a child, the outcome of a social engagement—its developmental "message"—is determined more by the quality and method of the child's participation than by ideas to which the child might be exposed.

If we want to train passive subjects of a totalitarian state, we should be careful to provide children only with relationships in which they are mindless recipients of indoctrination. If, on the other hand, we want democratic citizens, we should provide for them relationships in which they can think, argue, and freely make choices. Schools can provide such relationships for their students, and indeed must do so if they are to be effective forums for moral education. *This does not mean that schools should pretend to be value-neutral; or that teachers and administers should refrain from clear moral instruction and explanation.* Children need adult guidance. They also need to develop morally responsible habits. But reasoning can only strengthen and enlighten such habits. It is a necessary part of any moral education program worth launching.

Grounded in the progressive education tradition of John Dewey, and updated by the use of scientific moral development principles, is the "just community" approach to moral education.[21] The key to this approach is the transformation of the school into a participatory democracy where students share decision-making rights. The emphasis on school democracy reflects the belief that students must have first-hand experience in a just community if they are to develop values consistent with it. Active engagement in an egalitarian society is the surest way to acquire respect for others' rights. In contrast, the notion of an authoritarian school trying to instill principles of justice in its students is a contradiction in terms. The "moral atmosphere" of the school must be consistent with the values that it professes.

Schools in several parts of the country have taken this message seriously and have created forums for student participation in school governance. Typically there is a weekly "community meeting" to discuss school policies and rules. Students have a voice and a vote in these meetings. Topics can range from conduct in the halls to regulations regarding cheating. The purpose of such meetings is to impart a living sense of citizenship's rights and responsibilities. It is assumed that children who play a part in formulating rules will understand them better and be more willing to comply with them. They will also be more willing to enforce them, even if this means admonishing friends who violate the community's rules. Kohlberg writes, "In traditional schools, it is part of the teacher's role to be a policeman and for friends or students not to be. In a democratic school, it is not desirable for friends to be seen as policemen. It is, however, desirable for friends to have a feeling that at the center of their friendship is a mutual concern about fairness and the sense that their friendship and mutual loyalty exist in some balance within a larger moral community."[22]

When school norms are endorsed as much by students as by teachers, a "just community" has been created. A sense of group solidarity and communal loyalty is fostered. In such a "moral atmosphere", antisocial acts like stealing, violence, and vandalism become generally condemned and therefore less appealing. In addition, there is less of the individual alienation that often triggers such behavior. Turning students away from antisocial activities is another way in which a just community fosters moral growth.

An incident in one of Kohlberg's "just community" schools illustrates the way in which group solidarity based on moral norms can foster improved conduct and values among students.[23] The school had been plagued by numerous petty thefts, mostly by students stealing cash and other personal belongings from one another. In accord with the school's democratic goals, students and staff met regularly to discuss solutions to such disciplinary problems. The initial solution advanced by several students was to rigorously enforce punishments for anyone caught stealing. With strong student support, this was voted in as a school rule.

Stealing, however, continued unabated. An incident in which nine dollars was taken from a young girl's purse triggered off a new round of meetings on the theft problem. This time around, the issue was treated in a different manner. After many discussions, the group decided that stealing was a community as well as an individual problem and therefore that it should be dealt with through a community solution. Accordingly, the class voted that, unless the cash was returned to the girl by a certain date, all students and staff would be assessed a small sum to restore the stolen money. This kind of "theft insurance policy" gave all members of the school a direct interest in discouraging stealing within their community. One girl was quoted as saying, "If you want to rip off, rip off in your own time, not in school." (Of course one would hope that, with continued moral education, the girl's anti-stealing sentiments would generalize beyond the school to society at large). At least within the confines of the school, the "just community" strategy worked: stealing decreased dramatically once the new group solution was implemented. In fact, at the time that this incident was documented, two years had passed within the school without a single theft. No one can deny that this is an impressive achievement for a contemporary urban school.

Aside from creating a democratic community, schools adopting Kohlberg's approach to moral education make liberal use of the moral development techniques described above. These include teacher-led moral discussions, role-taking exercises, and curriculum materials that expose students to conflicts in fairness and moral choice.

The contrasts between Kohlberg's just community and Wynne's "great tradition" are as sharp as any that divide the educational world. Many of their respective goals stand in polar opposition to one another. Where Kohlberg sees equal participation, Wynne might see disorder; where Wynne sees high morale, Kohlberg might see empty jingoism. The moral agendas of both approaches have been set by their founders' ideologies, and these ideologies disagree from their root assumptions on up.

Such disagreement is not easily resolved, even by observing outcomes of the two approaches. This is because an outcome that one approach views as a success might be perceived by the other as a failure. Decline in student protest, for example, could well be a positive index of cohesiveness from Wynne's perspective but a negative index of apathy from Kohlberg's. How, then, may the effectiveness of either enterprise be objectively assessed?

The answer lies in identifiable areas of mutual concern shared by the two. Both approaches consider truancy, stealing, drug abuse, cruelty, violence, and vandalism to be wrongs that harm society and the youth that commit them. Both approaches agree that moral education should address these wrongs, and both claim that their own approach is ultimately the only effective way to do so. Unfortunately there are no good data in support of either claim. Here lies an opportunity for research. Ideologies aside, informed public decisions can be made on the very practical grounds that one or both approaches may alleviate the pressing problems that both agree must be alleviated. Then we may proceed to argue about the subtle (and not so subtle!) implications of the divergent ideologies.

As with any opposition, there are always points in between, as well as combinations drawn from both poles. Many school districts have adopted eclectic character education programs that take their principles and techniques from those advocated by both camps. At the present time the most widely adopted of these is a multiyear program designed by the American Institute for Character Education in San Antonio, Texas. This group has carefully crafted a set of materials combining moral reasoning techniques with some very traditional instruction in such basic American values as freedom, honesty, generosity, and fairness. Sections of the curriculum are devoted to conduct problems such as drug abuse, and teachers are advised to record students' behavioral changes from the beginning to the end of the year. Again, objective research is needed to gauge the effectiveness of this promising initiative, and the jury is still out for want of evidence.

Although we do not have enough evidence to make final judgments on current moral education programs, there are many conclusions that we can reasonably draw, based on our knowledge of children's morality. In fact, the theory and research documented by this book provide us with solid grounds for making recommendations concerning the types of moral education measures that should be implemented in our schools.

First, the overall goal of any program must be to help children reason autonomously about moral problems. No amount of rote learning or indoctrination will prepare children for the many diverse situations that they will face in life. The child must learn to find the moral issue in an ambiguous situation, to apply basic moral values to unfamiliar problems, and to create moral solutions when there is no one around to give the child direction. The only way to master these key challenges is to develop an autonomous ability to interpret, understand, and manage moral problems. Moral education programs must keep as their first goal the fostering of such an ability and above all must do nothing to hinder its development.

This does not mean, as many have wrongly assumed, that moral awareness programs should practice value neutrality. In fact, displays of values neutrality from teachers have an opposite effect to that intended. By failing to confront children with real values genuinely held, such displays engender in children an attitude of passive indifference—and even cynicism—towards the enterprise of moral choice. Why should a child bother working through a moral problem, or risk taking a stand, when the child's supposed moral mentor refrains from publicly doing so? To have a lasting effect, moral educators must confront children with basic values that are clearly stated and sincerely held.

We return to the principle of "respectful engagement." The child's own decision-making capacities must be respected and fostered if the child is to become an autonomous moral agent. But the child must not be given the message that whatever he decides is automatically right. The adult must *engage* the child with feedback, discussion, reasoning, and argumentation in order to convey the adult's position strongly and clearly. In an interaction characterized by respectful engagement, neither adult nor child can be passive. The adult, in fact, must encourage the child's active participation, not only to ensure the child's attentiveness but also to bring out the very decision-making capacities that the child must further develop. At the same time, the adult owes it both to herself and to the child to actively assert her own value commitments.

Nor do I believe that adults in our society need to agonize about what these values should be. Whether or not we take a universalist stance on morality, it is evident that many of our society's most fundamental values are widely enough shared for unhesitating intergenerational transmission. As I noted at the outset, none of us wants children who succumb to dishonesty, drugs, or cruel or antisocial behavior; and all of us want our children to endorse justice, legitimate authority, the needs of others, and their own responsibilities as citizens in a democratic society. Within this framework, there is plenty for us to argue about among ourselves, but there is also plenty that we can agree to impart to our children without ambiguity or hesitancy.

The essence of moral awareness is the ability to detect moral issues in complex social situations. In the Biblical parable of Jesus casting the money lenders from the temple, many simply may have seen a convenient place to change money after worship, where Jesus saw corruption and hypocrisy. Children naturally develop a certain degree of moral awareness through their social experience, but few children realize their full potential on their own. There is much that adults can do, directly and indirectly, to expand a child's moral awareness beyond its incipient state.

The moral education curricula discussed in this chapter can provide useful tools for enhancing children's moral awareness. In particular, the programs that have taken clear, unequivocal stands on moral choice while encouraging children's active participation are the ones that have proven most valuable. Moral discussion groups led by a trained teacher are perhaps the surest means of achieving these ends. In such groups, the teacher poses the problem and guides the discussion, but the children are encouraged by the peer dialogue to express their own views and to listen to each others' feedback. Children thus become engaged in the issue and are presented with, but not force-fed, peer feedback and an adult's moral guidance. This is the principle of respectful engagement in a collective educational setting.

Moral issues, however, can be found in many other school activities beyond specially designed moral education curricula. There is no need to confine moral discussion to topics that are explicitly designated "moral values." In fact, pointing out moral issues in previously unrecognized places can be exactly the kind of instruction children need to expand their moral awareness. It is this kind of instruction that can help them apply moral values to their everday lives rather than just to theoretical thinking. Here I would agree with William Bennett's suggestion that teachers identify for their students the values implicit in great works of literature, accounts of history, and so on.[24] But I would emphasize the importance of the Socratic method in so doing. If moral values are to stick, children's participation in the value dialogue must be encouraged. Little can be gained through one-way exposition and lecturing.

I have one further suggestion for fostering children's moral awareness in educational settings. To my knowledge this idea has never been attempted, but I see no reason why it could not be implemented in an extracurricular or other special school program. It would provide a mechanism for expanding children's moral awareness beyond the boundaries of their own limited social worlds. At the same time, it would engage children directly in an interpersonal encounter of great potential interest to them. Thus it would combine the breadth of a reading experience with the immediacy and appeal of interpersonal interaction.

Every community has within it men and women who have distinguished themselves through exemplary moral behavior.[25] Why not systematically bring such individuals into contact with our young? I can imagine no finer introduction to moral values in real life than exposure to individuals who have shown moral commitment and leadership in their own lives. Such "moral mentoring" can be inspiring as well as enlightening. It can enhance moral awareness by offering firsthand illustrations of the kinds of moral issues to which dedicated individuals respond. It also can enhance moral behavior by demonstrating how commitments to moral values can be translated into effective social action.[26]

Many schools and institutes have experimented with programs that bring working artists together with students. In both public and private education, there have been countless art workshops, seminars, master lessons, writers-in-residence programs, and other attempts to establish systematic classroom contact between students and people who make their careers in the arts. It is widely acknowledged that these have been among the most successful methods of instilling artistic skill as well as enduring motivation in the young.

"Moral mentors" could provide a similar educational function in the moral area. Of course they would not necessarily be labeled "moral mentors" per se: this could only lead to skepticism on the part of the student, and in any case few persons would be willing to announce themselves (or even privately consider themselves) as such. But they could be presented as leaders in, say, sheltering the homeless, healing the sick, caring for abandoned children, and so on, according to the moral problems addressed by the particular individuals participating. Presentations and discussions initially would be focused on these issues but would soon extend to the general principles and values that these issues represent.

I would expect that the ensuing exchanges would be among the deepest and liveliest of any in the child's moral education. As a consequence of such contacts, children also might become inspired to spend some of their free time in real helping activities, perhaps along the lines (or even as part of) the moral mentor's own enterprise. A child who spends some after school hours engaged in charitable activity will remember this experience far longer than a child who is simply told about such possibilities in school or at church. Inducting the child into action through inspirational example would encourage the child to assume genuine moral responsibility, the heart of moral character.

Notes

———•———

Preface

1. Coles, R. (1986) *The Moral Life of Children*. Boston: The Atlantic Monthly Press.

2. Kagan, J. and Lamb, S. (Eds.) (1987) *The Emergence of Morality in Young Children*. Chicago: University of Chicago Press.

Chapter One
MORAL CONCERNS FROM THE CHILD'S PERSPECTIVE

1. Stern, D. N. (1985) *The Interpersonal World of the Infant*. New York: Basic Books.

2. Stern, *The Interpersonal World of the Infant*.

3. Coles, *The Moral Life of Children*.

4. Hartshorne, H., and May, M. A. (1928–30) *Studies in the Nature of Character*. New York: Macmillan.

5. There is no evidence that children in the Hartshorne and May study were acting out of a sense of cooperation or childhood loyalty to their peers. But it is an old rule of science that investigators often miss what they are not prepared to find, and the Hartshorne/May investigation included no measures that could tap peer-oriented honor codes.

6. Piaget, J. (1932/1965) *The Moral Judgment of the Child*. New York: The Free Press.

Chapter Two
EMPATHY, SHAME, AND GUILT

1. Kagan, J. (1984) *The Nature of the Child*. New York: Basic Books.

2. Hoffman, M. (1982) Development of prosocial motivation: Empathy and guilt. In N. Eisenberg (Ed.), *The Development of Prosocial Behavior*. New York: Academic Press.

3. Hoffman, Development of prosocial motivation.

4. Hoffman, M. (1983). Empathy, guilt, and social cognition. In W. F. Overton (Ed.), *The Relationship Between Social and Cognitive Development*. Hillsdale, N.J.: L. Erlbaum Associates, pp. 12–13.

5. Feshbach, N. (1983) Sex differences in empathy and social behavior in children. In N. Eisenberg (Ed.), *The Development of Prosocial Behavior*. New York: Academic Press.

6. Eisenberg, N., and Miller, P. A. (1987) The relation of empathy to prosocial and related behaviors. *Psychological Bulletin, 94*, 100–131.

7. Samenow, S. E. (1984) *Inside the Criminal Mind*. New York: Random House.

8. Gibbs, J. (1987) Social processes in delinquency: The need to facilitate empathy as well as sociomoral reasoning. In W. Kurtines and J. Gewirtz (Eds.), *Moral Development Through Social Interaction*. New York: Wiley.

9. Samenow, *Inside the Criminal Mind*.

10. Radke-Yarrow, M., and Zahn-Waxler, C. (1984) Roots, motives, and patterns in children's prosocial behavior. In E. Staub, D. Bar-Tal, J. Karylowski, and J. Reykowski (Eds.), *Development and Maintainance of Prosocial Behavior: Interpersonal Perspectives on Positive Behavior*. New York: Plenum.

11. Mathews, K. A., Batson, C. D., Horn, J., and Rosenman, R. H. (1981) "Principles in his nature which interest him in the fortune of others . . . ": The heritability of empathic concern for others. *Journal of Personality, 49*, 237–247; see also Rushton, J. P., Fulker, D. W., Neale, M. C., Nias, D. K. B., and Eysenck, H. J. (1986) Altruism and aggression: The heritability of individual differences. *Journal of Personality and Social Psychology, 50*, 1192–1198.

12. Hoffman, M. (1981) Affective and cognitive processes in moral internalization. In E. T. Higgins, D. N. Ruble, and W. W. Hartup (Eds.), *Social Cognition and Social Behavior: Developmental Perspectives*. New York: Cambridge University Press.

13. Feshbach, Sex differences.

14. Gibbs, Social processes in delinquency.

15. Ibid., p. 313–314, quoting Samenow, *Inside the Criminal Mind*, p. 235.

16. Hoffman, *Affective and Cognitive Processes*.

17. Erikson, E. (1963) *Childhood and Society*, 2nd edition. New York: Norton.

18. Miller, D., and Swanson, G. (1960) *Inner Conflict and Defense*. New York: Holt, Rinehart, and Winston.

19. Hoffman, M. (1983). Empathy, guilt, and social cognition. In W. F. Overton (Ed.), *The Relationship Between Social and Cognitive Development*. Hillsdale, N.J.: L. Erlbaum Associates.

20. Hoffman, *Affective and Cognitive Processes*.

21. Radke-Yarrow and Zahn-Waxler, Roots, motives, and patterns.

22. Hoffman, *Affective and Cognitive Processes.*

23. Ibid.

24. Ibid.

25. Kagan, *The Nature of the Child.*

Chapter Three
LEARNING ABOUT JUSTICE THROUGH SHARING

1. Mueller, E., and Vandell, D. (1978) Infant-infant interaction. In J. Ososfsky (Ed.), *Handbook of Infancy.* New York: Wiley.

2. Piaget, J. (1962) *Play, Dreams, and Imitation.* New York: Norton.

3. Bronson, W. (1981) *Toddlers' Behavior with Agemates: Issues of Interaction, Cognition, and Affect.* Norwood, N.J.: Ablex Publishing.

4. Wilson, E. (1975) *Sociobiology.* Cambridge, Mass.: Harvard University Press.

5. Ugerel-Semin, R. (1952) Moral behavior and moral judgment of children. *Journal of Abnormal and Social Psychology, 47,* 463–474.

6. Eisenberg-Berg, N., Cameron, E., Tryon, K., and Dodez, R. (1981) Socialization of prosocial behavior in the preschool classroom. *Developmental Psychology, 17,* 773–782.

7. Bar-Tal, D. (1976) *Prosocial Behavior: Theory and Research.* New York: Wiley.

8. Damon, W. (1977) *The Social World of the Child.* San Francisco: Jossey-Bass, p. 66.

9. Ibid., pp. 81–87.

10. Eisenberg-Berg, N. (1979) The development of children's prosocial moral judgment. *Developmental Psychology, 15,* 128–137.

11. Damon, W. (1983) *Social and Personality Development.* New York: Norton.

12. Eisenberg, N. (Ed.) (1982) *The Development of Prosocial Behavior.* New York: Wiley.

13. Blasi, A. (1981) Bridging moral cognition and moral action: A critical review of the literature. *Psychological Bulletin, 88,* 593–637.

14. Froming, W. J., Allen, L., and Jensen, R. (1985) Altruism, Role-taking, and Self-awareness: The Acquisition of Norms Governing Altruistic Behavior. *Child Development, 56,* 1223–1228.

15. Damon, *The Social World of the Child.*

16. Eisenberg, *The Development of Prosocial Behavior.*

17. Murphy, L. (1937) *Social Behavior and Child Personality.* New York: Columbia University Press.

18. Bronson, *Toddlers' Behavior with Agemates.*

Chapter Four
PARENTAL AUTHORITY AND THE RULES OF THE FAMILY

1. Ainsworth, M. D., Blehar, M. C., Waters, E., and Wall, S. (1978) *Patterns of Attachment.* Hillsdale, N.J.: L. Erlbaum Associates.

2. Dunn, J., and Munn, P. (1985) Becoming a family member: Family conflict and the development of social understanding in the second year. *Child Development, 56,* 480–492; see also Dunn, J. (1987) The beginnings of moral understanding. In J. Kagan and S. Lamb (Eds.), *The Emergence of Morality in Young Children.* Chicago: University of Chicago Press, and Dunn, J., and Munn, P., (1986) Sibling quarrels and maternal intervention: Individual differences in understanding and aggression. *Journal of Child Psychology and Psychiatry, 27,* 583–595.

3. Dunn, The beginnings of moral understanding.

4. Ibid.

5. Dunn, J., and Munn, P. (1986) Siblings and the development of prosocial behavior. *International Journal of Behavioral Development, 9,* 265–294.

6. Ekman, P. (1984) Expression and nature of emotion. In K. R. Scherer and P. Ekman (Eds.), *Approaches to Emotion.* Hillsdale, N.J.: L. Erlbaum Associates.

7. Emde, R. Levels of meaning of infant emotions: A biosocial view. In W. A. Collins (Ed.), *Development of Cognition, Affect, and Social Relations* (Minnesota Symposium on Child Psychology, Vol. 13). Hillsdale, N.J.: L. Erlbaum Associates.

8. Sears, R. R., Maccoby, E. E., and Levin, H. (1957) *Patterns of Child Rearing.* Evanston, Ill.: Row Peterson.

9. Maccoby, E. E., and Martin, J. A. (1983) Socialization in the context of the family: Parent-child interaction. In P. H. Mussen (Ed.), *Handbook of Child Psychology* (Vol. 4). New York: Wiley.

10. Ibid.

11. Baldwin, A. (1948) Socialization and the parent-child relationship. *Child Developement, 19,* 127–136.

12. Baumrind, D. (1973) The development of instrumental competence through socialization. In A. D. Pick (Ed.), *Minnesota Symposium on Child Psychology* (Vol. 7). Minneapolis: University of Minnesota Press.

13. Ibid.

14. Ibid.

15. Ibid.

16. Ibid.

17. Ibid.

18. Baumrind, D. (1973) Note: Harmonious parents and their preschool children. *Develomental Psychology, 4,* 99–102.

19. Baumrind, D. (1989) Rearing competent children. In W. Damon (Ed.), *Child Development Today and Tomorrow.* San Francisco: Jossey-Bass.

20. Hoffman, M. L. (1967) Moral internalization, parental power, and the nature of parent-child interaction. *Developmental Psychology, 5,* 45–57.

21. Lepper, M. R., and Green, D. (1975) Turning play into work: Effects of surveillance and extrinsic reward on children's intrinsic motivation. *Journal of Personality and Social Psychology, 31,* 479–486.

22. Hoffman, M. L. (1977) Moral internalization. In L. Berkowitz (Ed.), *Advances in Experimental Social Psychology* (Vol. 10). New York: Academic Press.

23. Lepper, M. R. (1983) Social control processes, attributions of motivation, and the internalization of social values. In E. T. Higgins, D. N. Ruble, and W. W. Hartup (Eds.), *Social Cognition and Social Behavior: Developmental Perspectives.* New York: Cambridge University Press.

24. Lepper, Social control processes.

25. Flavell, J. (1982) *Cognitive Development.* Englewood Cliffs, N.J.: Prentice-Hall.

26. Baumrind, Rearing competent children.

27. Damon, W. (1977) *The Social World of the Child.* San Francisco: Jossey-Bass.

28. Ibid., pp. 174–175.

29. Ibid., p. 182.

30. Ibid., pp. 188–189.

31. Ibid., p. 192.

32. Ibid., p. 199.

33. Youniss, J. (1980) *Parents and Peers in Child Development.* Chicago: University of Chicago Press.

34. Whiting, B. B., and Whiting, J. W. M. (1975) *Children of Six Cultures: A Psychocultural Analysis.* Cambridge, Mass.: Harvard University Press.

35. Madsen, M. C. (1971) Developmental and cross-cultural differences in the cooperative and competetive behavior of young children. *Journal of Cross-Cultural Psychology, 2,* 365–371.

36. LeVine, R. A. (1980) Anthropology and child development. *New Directions for Child Development, 8,* 71–86.

37. Jiao, S., Ji, G., and Jing, Q. (1986) Comparative study of behavioral qualities of only children and sibling children. *Child Development, 57,* 357–361.

38. Ibid.

39. Ibid.

40. Edwards, C. P. (1987) Socialization in Kenya. In J. Kagan and S.

Lamb (Eds.), *The Emergence of Morality in Young Children.* Chicago: University of Chicago Press.

Chapter Five
INTERACTING AS EQUALS: FAIR PLAY IN THE PEER GROUP

1. Mueller, E., and Vandell, D. (1978) Infant-infant interaction. In J. Ososfsky (Ed.), *Handbook of Infancy.* New York: Wiley.

2. Davies, B. (1982) *Life in the Classroom and Playground: Accounts of Primary School Children.* London: Routledge and Kegan Paul.

3. Cairns, R. (1979) *Social Development: The Origins and Plasticity of Interchanges.* San Francisco: W. H. Freeman, p. 297.

4. Brazelton, T. B. (1976) Early parent-infant reciprocity. In V. C. Vaughn and T. B. Brazelton (Eds.), *The Family: Can It Be Saved?* Chicago: Yearbook Medical Publishers.

5. Davies, *Life in the Playground.*

6. Ibid.

7. Ibid.

8. Youniss, J. (1980) *Parents and Peers in Child Development.* Chicago: University of Chicago Press.

9. Ibid.

10. Ibid.

11. Ibid.

12. Berndt, T. (1987) The distinctive features of conversations between friends: Theories, research, and implications for sociomoral development. In W. Kurtines and J. Gewirtz (Eds.), *Moral Development Through Social Interaction.* New York: Wiley.

13. Ibid.

14. Ibid.

15. Davies, *Life in the Classroom and Playground.*

16. Ibid.

17. Gottman, J., and Parkhurst, J. (1980) A developmental theory and acquaintance processes. In W. A. Collins (Ed.), *Development of Cognition, Affect, and Social Relations* (Minnesota Symposium of Child Psychology, Vol. 13). Hillsdale, N.J.: L. Erlbaum Associates.

18. Davies, *Life in the Classroom and Playground.*

19. Damon, W. (1977) *The Social World of the Child.* San Francisco: Jossey-Bass, pp. 154–164.

20. Davies, *Life in the Classroom and Playground.*

21. Piaget, J. (1932/1965) *The Moral Judgment of the Child.* New York: The Free Press.

22. Hartup, W. (1979) The social worlds of childhood. *American Psychologist, 34,* 944–950.

23. Youniss, *Parents and Peers in Child Development.*

24. Ibid.

25. Gottman and Parkhurst, A developmental theory.

26. Mead, G. H. (1934) *Mind, Self, and Society.* Chicago: University of Chicago Press.

27. Flavell, J. H. et al. (1968) *The Development of Role-Taking and Communication Skills in Children.* New York: Wiley.

28. Selman, R. L. (1980) *The Growth of Interpersonal Understanding.* New York: Academic Press.

29. Borke, H. L. (1975) Piaget's mountains revisited: Changes in the egocentric landscape. *Developmental Psychology, 7,* 240–243.

30. Piaget, J. (1962) Comments on Vygotsky's critical remarks. In L. Vygotsky, *Thought and Language.* Cambridge, Mass.: M.I.T. Press.

Chapter Six
CULTURE, GENDER, AND MORALITY

1. MacIntyre, A. (1981) *After Virtue.* Notre Dame, Ind.: University of Notre Dame Press.

2. Klaus, M., and McDonald, L. (1985) *Relativism—Cognitive and Moral.* Chicago: University of Chicago Press.

3. Gilligan, C. (1982) *In a Different Voice: Psychological Theory and Women's Development.* Cambridge, Mass.: Harvard University Press.

4. Chodorow, N. *The Reproduction of Mothering: Psychoanalysis and the Sociology of Gender.* Berkeley: University of California Press.

5. Lewis, M., and Brooks-Gunn, J. (1979) *Social Cognition and the Acquisition of Self.* New York: Plenum.

6. Gilligan, *In a Different Voice.*

7. Ibid.

8. Ibid.

9. Ibid.

10. Ibid., pp. 26 and 28.

11. Ibid.

12. Eisenberg, N., and Miller, P. (1987) The relation of empathy to prosocial and related behaviors. *Psychological Bulletin, 101,* 91–119.

13. Piaget, J. (1932/1965) *The Moral Judgment of the Child.* New York: The Free Press.

14. Maccoby, E. E., and Jacklin, C. N. (1974) *The Psychology of Sex Differences.* Stanford, Calif.: Stanford University Press.

15. Staub, E. (1979) *The Development of Prosocial Behavior* (Vol. 2). New York: Academic Press.

16. Maccoby and Jacklin, *The Psychology of Sex Differences.*

17. Eagly, A. H., and Crowley, M. (1986) Gender and helping behavior: A meta-analytic review of the social-psychological literature. *Psychological Bulletin, 100,* 283–308.

18. Walker, L. (1983) Sex differences in the development of moral reasoning: A critical review. *Child Development, 54,* 1103–1141.

19. Edwards, C. P., and Whiting, B. B. (1980) Differential socialization of girls and boys in light of cross-cultural research. *New Directions for Child Development, 8,* 88–111.

20. Whiting, B. B., and Edwards, C. P. (1988) *Children of Different Worlds.* Cambridge, Mass: Harvard University Press.

21. Hugo, V. *Les Miserables.* Boston: Thomas Nelson and Son, p. 24.

22. Geertz, C. (1973) *The Interpretation of Cultures.* New York: Basic Books.

23. Shweder, R., Mahapatra, M., and Miller, J. (1987) Culture and moral development. In J. Kagan and S. Lamb (Eds.), *The Emergence of Morality in Young Children.* Chicago: University of Chicago Press.

24. Ibid.

25. Ibid.

26. Ibid., p. 71.

27. R. Gandhi, quoted in Turiel, E. (in press) Multifaceted social reasoning and educating for character, culture, and development. In L. Nucci and A. Higgins (Eds.), *Moral Development and Character Education: A Dialogue.* Chicago: National Society for the Study of Education Contemporary Issues Series.

28. Pasternak, B. (1959) *Dr. Zhivago.* Ann Arbor, Mich.: University of Michigan Press.

29. Edwards, C. P. (1987) Culture and the construction of moral values. In J. Kagan and S. Lamb (Eds.) *The Emergence of Morality in Young Children.* Chicago: University of Chicago Press.

30. LeVine, R. A., and White, M. I. (1986) *Human Conditions: The Cultural Basis of Educational Developments.* London: Routledge and Kegan Paul, p. 39.

31. Turiel, E. (1983) *The Development of Social Knowledge: Morality and Convention.* New York: Cambridge University Press.

32. Turiel, E., and Killen, M. (1988) Morality: Its structure, functions, and vagaries. In J. Kagan and S. Bloom (Eds.), *The Emergence of Morality.* Chicago: University of Chicago Press.

Chapter Seven
FOSTERING CHILDREN'S MORAL GROWTH

1. Hogan, R., Elmer, N., and Johnson, N. (1978) A socioanalytic theory of moral development. *New Directions for Child Development, 2,* 3–35.

2. Ibid.

3. Ibid.

4. Ibid.

5. Whiting, B. B., and Whiting, J. W. M. (1975) *Children of Six Cultures: A Psychocultural Analysis.* Cambridge: Harvard University Press.

6. Keniston, K., and the Carnegie Council on Children (1977) *All Our Children: The American Family Under Pressure.* New York: Harcourt Brace Jovanovich.

Chapter Eight
TEACHING VALUES IN THE SCHOOLS

1. Rath, L., Harmin, M., and Simon, S. (1966) *Values and Teaching: Working with values in the classroom.* Columbus, Ohio: Charles E. Merrill Publishing Company.

2. Ibid.

3. Ibid.

4. Ibid., p. 52.

5. Ibid., pp. 54-55.

6. Ibid., pp. 114-115.

7. Kohlberg, L. (1984) *Essays on Moral Development, Volume 2: The Psychology of Moral Development.* New York: Harper & Row.

8. Rest, J. (1983) Morality. In P. H. Mussen (Ed.), *Handbook of Child Psychology,* Vol. 3. New York: Wiley.

9. Lockwood, A. L. (1978) Effects of values clarification and moral development curricula on school-age subjects: A critical review of recent research. *Review of Education Research,* 48, 325-364.

10. Ibid.

11. Ibid.

12. Wynne, E. A. (1986) The great tradition in education: Transmitting moral values. *Educational Leadership,* 43, 4-9; see also Wynne, E. A. (1979) The declining character of American youth. *American Educator: The Professional Journal of the American Federation of Teachers,* 3, 29-32.

13. Wynne, The great tradition.

14. Wynne, Ibid.

15. Wynne, Ibid.

16. Bennett, W. J. (1980) The teacher, the curriculum, and values education. *New Directions for Higher Education,* 8, 27-34; Bennett, W. J. (1980) What value is values education? *American Educator,* 4, 31-32; Bennett, W. J., and Delattre, E. J. (1978) Moral education in the schools. *The Public Interest,* 50, 81-98; Bennett, W. J. and Delattre, E. J. (1979) A moral education: Some thoughts on how to best achieve it. *American Educator,* 3, 6-9.

17. Bennett and Delattre, A moral education.

18. Bennett, What value is values education?

19. Turiel, E. Multifaceted social reasoning and educating for character, culture, and development. (In press) In L. Nucci and A. Higgins (Eds.), *Moral Development and Character Education: A Dialogue*. Chicago: National Society for the Study of Education Contemporary Issues Series.

20. Kirkpatrick, J. J. (1979) The teaching of democratic values. *American Educator*, 3, 35–38.

21. Kohlberg, L. (1985) The just community in theory and practice. In M. Berkowitz and F. Oser (Eds.) *Moral Education*. Hillsdale, N.J.: L. Erlbaum Associates.

22. Kohlberg, The just community.

23. Power, C., and Reimer, J. (1978) Moral atmosphere: an educational bridge between moral judgment and action. In W. Damon (Ed.), *Moral Development: New Directions for Child Development*, Vol. 2. San Francisco: Jossey-Bass.

24. Bennett, What value is values education?

25. I can state this with some certainty, since, with Anne Colby, I am presently conducting a study of morally exemplary individuals. The intial phase of this study, aided by the Social Science Research Council, was dedicated to identifying moral exemplars who are alive in the world today (see note 26, below). Our criteria were quite stringent. By our definition, a moral exemplar shows: 1) A sustained commitment to moral principles; 2) A consistent tendency to act in accordance with these principles; 3) A willingness to affirm (rather than deny or misrepresent) one's acts; 4) A willingness to risk personal well-being for the sake of one's moral principles; 5) A talent for inspiring others to moral action; 6) A sense of humility rather than grandiosity or egotism; and 7) A dedication and responsiveness to the needs of others. In order to identify living persons who exemplify these criteria, we surveyed moral scholars with a wide diversity of ideological, religious, political, and cultural beliefs. Despite the stringency of our criteria, these scholars were able to name a very large number of persons who fit. As we investigated further, names of moral exemplars turned up virtually everywhere. We were, in fact, surprised and encouraged at the omnipresence of individuals who have dedicated their lives—sometimes publicly, more often quietly—to carrying out moral principles.

26. Damon, W., and Colby, A. (1987) Social influence and moral change. In W. Kurtines and J. Gewirtz (Eds.), *Moral Development Through Social Interaction*. New York: Wiley.

Index